Pathways to Success

Case Studies for
Mainstreaming Corporate Sustainability

Suzanne Farver, ALM, JD

ISBN-13: 978-1-60427-171-3

Printed and bound in the U.S.A. Printed on acid-free paper.

10 9 8 7 6 5 4 3 2 1

For Library of Congress Cataloging-in-Publication Data, please visit the WAV section of the publisher's website at www.jrosspub.com/wav.

Phone: (954) 727-9333
Fax: (561) 892-0700
Web: www.jrosspub.com

This book is dedicated to sustainability professionals around the world who have demonstrated that you can do well by doing good. The late Ray Anderson lived by this motto—and we have to thank him for his leadership. To those industry leaders who have pushed their competitors to improve their business practices and to move policies into more positive and responsible directions for this planet— we are indebted to you. Thank you to all who have been brave enough to show us the way—and to the believers who support them.

CONTENTS

PREFACE

This is a companion book to *Mainstreaming Corporate Sustainability: Using Proven Tools to Promote Business Success,* which is a basic introduction to incorporating environmental and social responsibility into the management and strategy for a successful and profitable corporation.

Each chapter of this book coordinates with the chapters of the textbook, providing cases for different companies on each subject—from stakeholder engagement to supply chain management and reporting. I've chosen exemplary companies for each subject to help the reader better understand the concepts and see how it has successfully been applied by an actual operating corporation.

Each chapter has a broad overview of the case company, followed by suggested extra resources regarding the subject and how to find more information about the company's current reporting and performance. The information changes from year to year, so I've tried to keep the references general enough to provide access to what's happening on the ground when you read this book.

Companies change and grow over time, and their leadership direction for sustainability can change too. Not all companies perform well in all areas of sustainability, and you'll find that each of the companies here has challenges in one area or another. That is part of what makes sustainability such a tough field, and it is always a work in progress. There are forever new targets and new challenges.

The purpose of this book and the parent textbook is to provide a solid overview of the resources available to today's business leaders. Who are some of the leading voices in this field? What tools have they used, and what do they have to offer? What are some of the toughest challenges? How do you begin this journey for your own company? How do you avoid being overwhelmed by the volume of material offered on the subject?

Although there are still many new ideas and approaches being developed, the basic topics have become well established in the field of sustainability. Seeing how these principles have been applied in the industry can help you to see how they can be used for your own company or organization. The end of each chapter includes suggestions for further reading to help you dig more deeply into particular areas of interest.

ACKNOWLEDGMENTS

This book is the culmination of the efforts of many years of preparation, and without the help and support of my family and friends, it would not have come to fruition.

I have had many mentors along the way, but there are a few in particular who have stood out and supported this work. Amory Lovins at the Rocky Mountain Institute remains a visionary and exemplar in so many ways. His thirst for knowledge, attention to detail, and expansive respect for nature and humankind are an inspiration to all. His humor and kindness are without match.

To my co-instructor Matt Gardner, thank you for many years of collaboration in our class at Harvard Extension School. And to Zeina Eyceoz, thank you for taking on my responsibilities in the class beginning in 2017, allowing me to finish this book and to move on to new responsibilities at Presidio Graduate School.

To my colleagues at Presidio Graduate School, I am indebted for your leadership and camaraderie. We have been through many educational challenges together, and I thank you for your support as we have found new pathways for our school to thrive. Special thanks to Dariush Rafinejad, our provost, who has brought our curriculum to new heights; to Donna LaSala, our talented and exuberant MPA faculty leader; to Eric Cetnarski, who has been an undaunted leader of our staff while I served as interim president; and to Mary Kay Chess, former dean at our Seattle campus, who provides leadership, love, and support to so many. You have all propped me up when I needed it, and I am eternally grateful. I couldn't have completed this book without your great work helping to manage our school.

To all of you on this journey, thank you for your fellowship and solidarity. We have an enormous responsibility to care for this earth and to leave it a better place for our children's children and beyond.

LIST OF APPENDICES

ABOUT THE AUTHOR

Suzanne Farver, ALM, JD, has spent her career leading organizations toward more responsible management and has a strong track record of building consensus and emulating vision. She holds a BA in economics from Grinnell College (Phi Beta Kappa), a JD from the University of Denver, and an ALM in environmental management from Harvard University Extension School (class marshal).

Her educational work includes teaching Corporate Sustainability Strategy at Harvard University Extension School, a course she helped develop in the fall of 2010. In 2013, she published the first edition of *Mainstreaming Corporate Sustainability: Using Proven Tools to Promote Business Success*, which serves as a textbook for the Harvard class and other universities across the globe. The book helps business administrators promote profitable strategies to incorporate social and environmental solutions into their firm's strategic plans.

Suzanne's nonprofit management includes serving as finance chair for the Rocky Mountain Institute (RMI) board during its merger with the Carbon War Room and hiring of a new executive director, Jules Kortenhorst. During that time, RMI tripled in size and impact, and continues now as a leading organization helping the business community to drive energy savings and reduce carbon emissions worldwide.

Since 2006 Suzanne has served on the board of Presidio Graduate School (PGS), including board chair from 2015 to 2018, during a time of enormous transition for the school. Under Suzanne's leadership, the school entered a new partnership with Amity University, a leading nonprofit international university with campuses worldwide. This new venture greatly increases the impact of the

PGS mission, which includes promoting business practices that recognize the importance of social justice. PGS awards MBAs and MPAs who are focused on sustainable management principles and was mentioned in *The New York Times* as the best MBA program to attend "if you want to change the world."

CHAPTER **1**

INTRODUCTION TO SUSTAINABILITY

What is corporate sustainability? Most sustainability experts today argue that corporate sustainability involves three basic resource areas that are impacted by any company: environmental, social, and economic. Some refer to these as the three responsibilities or the triple bottom line. You may sometimes see other factors being included in the definition for sustainability: governance, transparency, local engagement, or longevity. How do you drive a company toward responsibility in these areas? In this book we offer you a chance to dig deeply into various companies that practice corporate sustainability and how it helps their businesses thrive. But in this chapter, we'll try to stay at the thirty-thousand-foot level and attempt to understand what corporate sustainability means from a broad perspective.

The Brundtland Commission defined sustainable development as follows—it is a broad definition that doesn't mention the specifics of environment or social well-being (Bärlund 2004–05):

> *Development that meets the needs of current generations without compromising the ability of future generations to meet their own needs.*

The United Nations Global Compact defines corporate sustainability in the following manner—note they add ethics to the mix (UNGC 2014):

> *Corporate sustainability is a company's delivery of long-term value in financial, environmental, social, and ethical terms.*

In *Mainstreaming Corporate Sustainability*, the following definition of corporate sustainability is offered (Farver 2013):

> *Corporate sustainability means balancing environmental stewardship, social well-being, and economic prosperity while driving toward a goal of long-term success for the health of the company and its stakeholders. A sustainable corporation is transparent in its management of these responsibilities and is held accountable to its stakeholders for its results.*

Which definition makes the most sense to you? Can you find other definitions that may clarify the appropriate values and at the same time provide guidance to an organization to achieve those values?

Various experts prescribe steps that must be taken to achieve corporate sustainability. Having stepping-stones and guidelines can help to drive sustainability and incorporate it into a company's management systems. We will delve into some of these frameworks throughout this book, but for now, just know that it is helpful to have guidance and that there are choices available that can be customized to a particular company's culture and values.

SUSTAINABILITY RANKINGS

There are many sustainability ranking systems worldwide, and these rankings can help to determine the leaders in this field. Or do they? Sometimes you may be surprised to see who is leading in these lists.

Newsweek publishes one of the most popular sustainability lists. It has been published annually since 2009 (well, almost annually—they missed 2013 due to some system changes). They have partnered with various analytical firms, including Trucost and Sustainalytics, to formulate their listings; their most recent partner being Corporate Knights. The Newsweek Green Rankings 2014 list raised some eyebrows. Former top ten companies were shuffled to lower rankings and others fell off the list entirely.

The reason behind this shift was due to the methodology of the ranking— that is, the types of information collected and the weight given to each factor. Newsweek had been tweaking its methodology over the years, but in 2014 it made a major shift when it even changed which types of information were most important for the rankings. They seem to have settled in now with a methodology that has been used for the past three years. The following indicators were retrieved from their website (Newsweek 2016a):

- Indicator 1: Combined Energy Productivity—Weight: 15%
- Indicator 2: Combined Greenhouse Gas (GHG) Productivity—Weight: 15%
- Indicator 3: Combined Water Productivity—Weight: 15%
- Indicator 4: Combined Waste Productivity—Weight: 15%
- Indicator 5: Green Revenue Score—Weight: 20%
- Indicator 6: Sustainability Pay Link—Weight: 10%
- Indicator 7: Audited Environmental Metrics—Weight: 5%
- Indicator 8: Sustainability Board Committee—Weight: 5%

The top ten companies chosen by Newsweek for 2016 are shown in Table 1.1:

Table 1.1 Newsweek Top Ten for 2016 (Newsweek 2016b)

1. Shire PLC	Ireland	Health Care
2. Reckitt Benckiser Group PLC	Britain	Consumer Staples
3. BT Group PLC	Britain	Telecommunication Services
4. Swisscom AG	Switzerland	Telecommunication Services
5. Essilor International S.A.	France	Health Care
6. Nike, Inc.	United States	Consumer Discretionary
7. Unilever	Britain	Consumer Staples
8. Sky PLC	Britain	Consumer Discretionary
9. Siemens AG	Germany	Industrials
10. Schneider Electric SE	France	Industrials

There is also an interesting commentary on Newsweek's methodology shift in an article on GreenBiz.com by GreenBiz chairman and chief executive editor, Joel Makower. In his article, he notes that the new methodology is more data driven and quantitative, which allows for better tracking and checking of results. However, this approach eliminates some of the qualitative analysis that may inform some of the better choices. In addition, it can eliminate the context of some of the data. He uses the example of comparing water efficiency between IBM, largely a hardware manufacturer, and Adobe, whose products are largely based in the cloud. Such a comparison would put IBM's results at a disadvantage (Makower 2014).

Another interesting part to the story is that Corporate Knights, one of the partners in producing the Newsweek list, also publishes its own sustainability rankings, and this is a completely different list! See their results in Table 1.2.

Table 1.2 Corporate Knights Top 10 for 2016 (Corporate Knights 2016)

1. BMW	Germany	Automobiles
2. Dassault Systèmes	France	Software
3. Outotec	Finland	Construction and Engineering
4. Commonwealth Bank of Australia	Australia	Banks
5. adidas	Germany	Textiles, Apparel, and Luxury Goods
6. Enagas	Spain	Gas Utilities
7. Danske Bank	Denmark	Banks
8. StarHub	Singapore	Wireless Telecommunication Services
9. Reckitt Benckiser Group	United Kingdom	Household Products
10. City Developments	Singapore	Real Estate Mgmt. and Development

The methodology for the Corporate Knights list appears to be much more customized among industry groups, taking KPIs (key performance indicators) from each industry and making sure that the company in that group performs and reports well against its peers. You can see more details on the Corporate Knights website, but the summary here is taken directly from their webpage (Corporate Knights 2015):

- *First screen*: sustainability disclosure
  - The first screen eliminates companies that are not keeping pace with the sustainability reporting trends in their specific industry
- *Second screen*: F-score
  - The Piotroski F-score consists of nine individual [profitability] tests
- *Third screen*: product category
  - Companies in certain product categories such as tobacco are eliminated; others, such as defense, are eliminated if their primary business is weapons production
- *Fourth screen*: sanctions
  - A calculation of sanctions paid is made to determine if a company should remain on the list
- Previous year Global 100 constituents
  - Global 100 companies from the previous year are added if they are not in the bottom quartile of their Global Industry Classification Standard (GICS) Industry Group on the fourth screen (sanctions)
- The Global 100 shortlist
  - All companies on the shortlist are scored on a percent rank basis against their GICS Industry peers on the priority KPIs for their respective GICS Industry Group
- The Global 100
  - The Global 100 consists of the companies with the top overall score in each GICS sector; in order to match the industry composition of the benchmark, each sector is assigned a fixed number of slots in the Global 100

Many of you may also be familiar with the Carbon Disclosure Project (CDP) and the Dow Jones Sustainability Index (DJSI). These are two highly respected rating systems, but they come at it once again from different perspectives and use different methodologies. The CDP focuses mostly upon carbon emissions and how companies are reducing their carbon footprint, but they do consider other environmental factors and whether companies are considering the overall environmental risks in a responsible manner for their industry. Their ratings are also focused more within industries; they do not publish an overall list of leaders. You can find a link to their most recent report in the reference list at the end of this chapter (CDP 2015).

The DJSI is compiled by ROBECOSAM, and is a combination of answers to questions submitted to the companies as well as feedback from media and other stakeholders. At least half of the questions are "industry-specific risks and opportunities that focus on economic, environmental, and social challenges and trends that are particularly relevant to companies within that industry." The feedback part of the analysis includes investigating labor disputes, human rights violations, or environmental issues, any of which can negatively impact a company's bottom line. The DSJI Index Committee reviews the analysis before the final list is compiled (ROBECOSAM n.d.a.).

Table 1.3 shows the top ten from the DJSI list of leading companies for 2015.

Table 1.3   Dow Jones Sustainability Index 2015 (ROBECOSAM n.d.b.)

1. Peugeot SA	France	Automobiles and Components
2. Westpac Banking Corp	Australia	Banks
3. CNH Industrial NV	United Kingdom	Capital Goods
4. SGS SA	Switzerland	Commercial and Professional Services
5. LG Electronics Inc	Republic of Korea	Consumer Durables and Apparel
6. InterContinental Hotels Group PLC	United Kingdom	Consumer Services
7. UBS Group AG	Switzerland	Diversified Financials
8. Thai Oil PCL	Thailand	Energy
9. METRO AG	Germany	Food and Staples Retailing
10. Coca-Cola HBC AG	Switzerland	Food, Beverage, and Tobacco

Yet another type of sustainability ranking is performed by SustainAbility and Globescan and has a 20-year history. Their list is developed from surveys of over 800 experts in the field rather than from collecting specific data about each company. Their list of experts includes nongovernmental organizations (NGOs), businesses, governments, and academia across 84 countries. Hence, their list is very much dependent upon a company's reputation and how the company influences its peers in the industry. Their listing includes many of those found on other lists, but you can see that the top ten is quite different from the previous listings. The following is the list of the top ten global companies from this year's surveys. You can see that Unilever has wide recognition among its peers for its sustainability efforts (GlobeScan and SustainAbility 2016). Unilever will be one of the case studies later in this book.

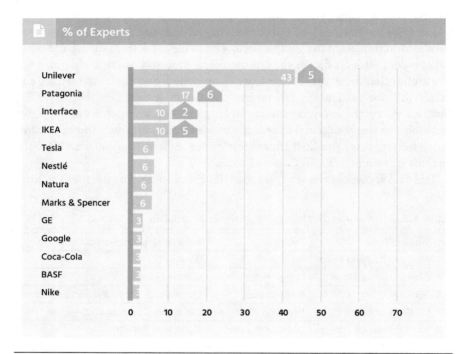

Figure 1.1   GlobeScan and SustainAbility top ten list (Reprinted from The 2016 Sustainability Leaders: A GlobeScan/SustainAbility Survey with permission of GlobeScan and SustainAbility.)

The point of emphasizing this detail is that choosing the best in sustainability rankings can have significantly different results depending upon your priorities. So what priorities are appropriate? How do you choose the right priorities, and how do you weigh them?

The Global Institute for Sustainability Ratings (GISR) has compiled a *ratings hub*—a comprehensive list of data on environmental, social, and governance (ESG) rankings from around the world. As you weigh the questions from this introduction, you may find it valuable to consult its website and view the data it has collected on the various rating systems (GISR 2016).

In this book we try to provide some important background materials and help you develop the critical skills that will assist you in making these choices.

The world needs qualified professionals who are asking the right questions in their organizations to promote sustainability across industry fields. Understanding how methodologies are created and reported upon is part of that requirement.

The goal of this chapter is to get you to think about the differing methodologies of these raters. Do the various lists truly reflect all areas of sustainability? Think about how they approach the environment (including resource use, CO_2 emissions, and toxic waste), health and safety of the workforce, social and environmental concerns in the supply chain, and governance (including diversity on the board of directors as well as executive compensation). Financial performance weighs in as well, of course. After all, it is hard to do good for society and the environment if you aren't still in business.

CASE STUDIES

This book presents a variety of case studies in our efforts to better understand how sustainability principles are applied in practice. In this first chapter, we do not have a case, but instead we ask some general questions about sustainability for you to research and consider.

In the next chapter, we investigate the business case for sustainability, and we give you a few examples from case companies that we present in this book. How does a company justify its investment in sustainability measures? What types of metrics are involved, and what is the driver for making changes from previous practices?

In later chapters we examine the various aspects of sustainability and how these areas work together to embed sustainability into a company. In each chapter we also try to loop back to the business case so that you can have an opportunity to see how different companies find value in sustainability. Why do they embrace the investments in sustainability measures? What kinds of metrics do they use to ensure they are making progress? The cases cover a variety of industries, including apparel, consumer products, manufacturing, retail, energy production, and real estate management.

The goal here is to provide you with a number of sustainability exemplars—those companies that have taken sustainability seriously and are applying it in every area of their business. They are truly mainstreaming sustainability into their companies and making it a priority for every department. They have found metrics to measure the value of sustainability initiatives and have tracked how that value has translated into profits and increased customer loyalty. The reasons for undertaking sustainability measures vary from company to company.

You will have the opportunity to evaluate and understand those motivations by closely investigating each company.

ADDITIONAL RESOURCES

The following are the suggested resources for this chapter:

- "UN Global Compact Guide to Corporate Sustainability." (2015). Available at: https://www.unglobalcompact.org/library/1151.
- Carbon Disclosure Project. "CDP Global Climate Change Report 2015: At the tipping point?" Available at: https://www.cdp.net/en/research/global -reports/global-climate-change-report-2015.
- "Six Growing Trends in Corporate Sustainability." (2013). Available at: https://www.ey.com/us/en/services/specialty-services/climate-change -and-sustainability-services/six-growing-trends-in-corporate-sustainability.
- Why Sustainability Rankings Matter (blog, Allen White, *MIT Sloan Management Review*). Available at: https://sloanreview.mit.edu/article/ why-sustainability-ratings-matter/.

QUESTIONS FOR THIS CHAPTER

1. *Definition of sustainability*: If you were the CEO of a large corporation, which definition of sustainability would you choose? How might it be different for a smaller company? Are there other definitions you can find that would be useful to consider here? If you find a definition you like, support your argument by informing your cohort regarding the qualifications of your source and how it would be an effective definition for a modern multinational corporation.
2. *Brand reputation*: Take a look at one or two of the rating systems mentioned earlier. How do various companies rate in one list versus another? Can you explain the difference in rating based upon the rating system's methodology? Are there other rating lists that you can find that might complement one of those presented here?
3. *Setting goals*: Spend some time reviewing some of the additional resources suggested at the end of this chapter. You don't have to read everything; rather, skim over the various materials and find one that interests you most and dig into it a bit. What strikes you as important

regarding sustainability for a corporation at this point—and why?
What are some of the biggest challenges for a company pursuing sustainability, and what kinds of initial steps need to be taken to start the
sustainability journey?

REFERENCES

Bärlund, K. (2004–2005). "Sustainable Development—Concept and Action."
United Nations Economic Commission for Europe. Retrieved from: http://
www.unece.org/oes/nutshell/2004-2005/focus_sustainable_development
.html.
Carbon Disclosure Project (CDP). (2015). "CDP Global Climate Change Report 2015: At the Tipping Point?" Retrieved from: https://www.cdp.net/en/
research/global-reports/global-climate-change-report-2015.
Corporate Knights. (2015). "2016 Global 100 Methodology." Corporate Knights.
Retrieved from: http://www.corporateknights.com/reports/2016-global-100/
2016-global-100-methodology-14419904/):/.
Corporate Knights. (2016). "2016 Global 100 Results." Corporate Knights, Winter Issue. Retrieved from: http://www.corporateknights.com/magazines/
2016-global-100-issue/2016-global-100-results-14533333/.
Farver, S. (2013). *Mainstreaming Corporate Sustainability: Using Proven Tools to
Promote Business Success.* Cotati, CA: Greenfix, LLC.
Global Institute for Sustainability Ratings (GISR). (2016). "Corporate Sustainability (ESG) Ratings, Rankings and Indexes." Retrieved from: http://rate
sustainability.org/hub/index.php/search/.
GlobeScan and SustainAbility. (2016). "The 2016 Sustainability Leaders: A
GlobeScan/SustainAbility Survey." Available from: https://globescan.com/
the-2016-gss-sustainability-leaders-report/.
Makower, J. (2014). "Do Newsweek's green rankings still matter?" Green
Biz.com. Retrieved from: https://www.greenbiz.com/blog/2014/06/05/do
-newsweeks-green-rankings-still-matter.
Newsweek. (2016a). "2016 Newsweek green rankings: FAQ." Retrieved from:
https://www.newsweek.com/2016-newsweek-green-rankings-faq-464496.
Newsweek. (2016b). "Top Ten Green Companies in the World." Retrieved from:
https://www.newsweek.com/green-2016/top-10-green-companies-world
-2016.
ROBECOSAM. (n.d.a.). "Corporate Sustainability Assessment." Retrieved July 25,
2016, from: http://www.sustainability-indices.com/sustainability-assessment/
corporate-sustainability-assessment.jsp.

ROBECOSAM. (n.d.b.). "Industry Group Leaders 2015." Retrieved July 25, 2016, from: http://www.robecosam.com/en/sustainability-insights/about-sustain ability/corporate-sustainability-assessment/industry-group-leaders.jsp.

United Nations Global Compact (UNGC). (2014). "Guide to Corporate Sustainability: Shaping a Sustainable Future." New York: United Nations Global Compact. Retrieved from: https://www.unglobalcompact.org/docs/publications/UN_Global_Compact_Guide_to_Corporate_Sustainability.pdf.

CHAPTER 2

MAKING THE BUSINESS CASE
FOR SUSTAINABILITY

EXAMINING THE BUSINESS CASE

In this chapter we will investigate some of the companies rated highly on the sustainability ranking lists that you compared in the last chapter. How are these companies making a business case for their sustainability efforts? What arguments are they using to justify their investment in environmental and social responsibility? What benefits are they reaping from these investments, and how could they improve their efforts? These are the kinds of questions we will investigate throughout this book from the various perspectives of sustainability, but in this chapter we focus specifically upon making the business case for sustainability.

The MIT/BCG surveys mentioned in the "Business Case" chapter of *Mainstreaming Corporate Sustainability* can be helpful in understanding the mindsets of company executives who are driving sustainability. There are links to these surveys at the end of this chapter. These surveys summarize the tactics of companies who are actively engaged in sustainability, compared to those who are interested but may be standing on the sidelines. The most successful engagers are managing their companies by mainstreaming sustainability into their strategies and decisions. Those on the sidelines may aspire to managing resources and people more responsibly, but they have no organized effort to do so.

Making a business case for sustainability involves measuring the risks and benefits of your efforts. Sometimes those efforts can be quantified in financial terms by asking pertinent questions. How much will we save by recycling this waste versus sending it to the landfill? Will we need a partner who is interested in that product for recycling in order to better facilitate that practice? Alternatively, how much of an investment will it take to change the light bulbs in our hotel, and how soon will we see a payback? What might be the possible challenges for guests or for our staff?

Sometimes the metrics aren't so easily quantifiable, yet they need to be accounted for by some sort of customized score. For example, investing in a local community education program may be foreseen to improve the local employee pool, but how can the benefits be measured? How long would it take to begin to see the benefits? Or would there be short-term benefits to attract top talent if those individuals felt their families would have good educational opportunities? Companies often draft their own customized scorecards to track progress in these areas.

At other times, insurance costs can help to pin a value on sustainability efforts. Reinsurance companies are helping insurance companies project the costs of damage from stronger storms and climate change. As mentioned in a 2013 MIT/BCG survey, Swiss Re has helped cities such as Hull in the United Kingdom project the increased cost of damage from its inaction on climate change. They found that losses could be reduced by up to 65 percent through 2030 if they retrofitted buildings, strengthened sea defenses, and improved building codes (MIT/BCG 2013).

In addition, the context of the particular facility may be relevant. For example, for a beverage company or a paper mill, water would be an important resource. Managing that water supply may vary depending on the particular aspects of the facility's watershed, pollution conditions, or regulations. For a company with facilities all over the world, emphasis on certain resources may therefore vary from facility to facility.

Overall, each company will have to develop its own business case, depending on the forces that are relevant to that company. For resource extracting companies, availability of scarce commodities may drive improvements. For consumer goods, it may be customer pressure toward a more responsible supply chain. For a hospital, it may be creating a healthy and clean environment for its patients.

In this chapter you will compare how various companies have made the business case for sustainability. If you were an executive in one of these companies, what types of information would you present to the corporate leaders to improve these measures and drive them into the company's culture and practices?

Examples of the business case can come from the companies themselves. Nestlé is found at the top of many sustainability rankings and is often cited as an example of using the shared-value concept described by Michael Porter and Mark Kramer in their *Harvard Business Review* article (2011). Nestlé has found that as its business grows, it has become increasingly dependent on a reliable supply of raw materials. The company supports its suppliers in a way that not only benefits the suppliers but also provides a less expensive and more dependable supply to Nestlé itself. It now works with more than 600,000 suppliers of dairy, cocoa, and coffee and has removed intermediaries from its supply chain—lowering costs and improving traceability. This is an important concern in today's social-media-controlled market, where food safety issues can spread like wildfire. Nestlé has also improved the working conditions and farming practices of the growers, benefiting the local communities in which the company interacts. This will also protect Nestlé in the future when climate change and growing population create new pressures on the supply of these goods.

For beverage companies, water and energy are increasing concerns. Since most of the growth in new markets for these companies lies in developing countries, some beverage companies are working with local communities to enhance water quality and supply. This not only improves their license to operate in these communities but also ensures a quality water supply for their own bottling operations. PepsiCo received an award in 2012 for its efforts to reduce water efficiency across its operations. These efforts included improving agricultural use of water in India as well as providing assistance to its manufacturing operations to reduce water usage. Coca-Cola has developed a water recovery system for its manufacturing plants that could reduce water use by up to 35 percent (Environmental Leader 2012).

Beer companies are beginning to understand these concerns, and they are starting to emphasize water and energy use in their sustainability reports. SABMiller, for example, has collaborated with the World Wildlife Fund and Coca-Cola to develop partnerships with local governments to assess the risks to water resources and to create action plans to mitigate those risks (SAB-Miller 2011).

How could these companies continue to improve their performance, and how can they justify the investments needed to support these programs? These are the types of questions that will be investigated at the end of this chapter.

Here are a few suggested companies to consider, including some of the companies we will be focusing on in this book:

- BMW
- Coca-Cola Company
- Gap
- IBM
- Interface
- Levi Strauss
- Nestlé

- Patagonia
- PepsiCo
- Unilever

For this chapter, please take a look at one or two of these companies' financial/sustainability reports. Your investigation should include how you think they have developed a business case for sustainability. What types of things are they doing well regarding their environmental and social performance, and what kind of a business case are they making for what they have planned and accomplished? How could their business case be improved? What types of goals would you like to see on their list? What areas do you think are being ignored, and what is being overemphasized? Is there any *green-washing* going on? Put on your critical thinking cap, and see if you can determine how the business case for these companies could be improved.

ADDITIONAL RESOURCES

MIT Sloan Management Review and Boston Consulting Group Surveys—these are published roughly annually and are conducted with leading executives:

- MIT-BCG 2017 Survey—"Corporate Sustainability at a Crossroads": https://sloanreview.mit.edu/projects/corporate-sustainability-at-a-crossroads/#chapter-9.
- MIT-BCG 2016 Survey—"Investing for a Sustainable Future"—Executive Summary and Report: https://sloanreview.mit.edu/projects/investing-for-a-sustainable-future/.
- MIT-BCG 2015 Survey—"Joining Forces: Collaboration and Leadership for Sustainability": https://sloanreview.mit.edu/projects/joining-forces/.

Natural Capital Solutions has collected a number of studies on the business case, and they are summarized in this publication along with links to the studies themselves. This is a handy guide to gather a number of perspectives:

- Sustainability Pays: https://natcapsolutions.org/wp-content/uploads/2017/02/businesscasereports.pdf.

Harvard Business Review published a groundbreaking article on shared value by Porter and Kramer in 2006. This is a sequel and update to that article. We'll look at it again later in this book, but I am providing it to you here because it presents an excellent basis for the argument of the business case for sustainability:

- Porter, M. and M. Kramer. (2011). "Creating Shared Value": https://hbr.org/2011/01/the-big-idea-creating-shared-value.

QUESTIONS FOR THIS CHAPTER

1. *Challenges and successes*: What challenges have companies faced when developing their business case for sustainability? What are some of the best successes you can find? Are there different approaches you can see that help one company over another to create their business case?
2. *Existing methods*: Take a bit of time to read some of the materials about one of the companies mentioned in this chapter. How have they made their own business case for the sustainability measures they have implemented? Investigate how their sustainability investments could be improved by the business case methods that were presented in this chapter. How can they use these methods to improve their sustainability goals and performance record? What types of goals would you like to see on their list? What areas do you think are being ignored, and what is being overemphasized?
3. *Other information*: Can you find other information that would help to make a business case for sustainability for one of these companies? You might look through the MIT/BCG studies on the business case posted at the end of the chapter. Which examples could be applied to the company you've chosen to support investments in sustainability programs?

REFERENCES

Environmental Leader. (2012). "Pepsi Water Efficiency Wins Plaudits." Environmental Leader. Retrieved from: https://www.environmentalleader.com/2012/08/pepsi-water-efficiency-wins-plaudits/.

MIT Sloan Management Review and The Boston Consulting Group (MIT/BCG). (2009). "The Business of Sustainability." Cambridge, MA: Massachusetts Institute of Technology. Available from: https://sloanreview.mit.edu/article/special-report-measuring-to-manage/.

MIT Sloan Management Review and The Boston Consulting Group (MIT/BCG). (2011). "Sustainability: The 'Embracers' Seize Advantage." Cambridge, MA: Massachusetts Institute of Technology. Available from: https://sloanreview.mit.edu/projects/sustainability-the-embracers-seize-advantage/.

MIT Sloan Management Review and The Boston Consulting Group (MIT/BCG). (2013). "Sustainability's Next Frontier: Walking the Talk on the Sustainability Issues That Matter Most." Cambridge, MA: Massachusetts Institute of Technology. Available from: https://sloanreview.mit.edu/projects/sustainabilitys-next-frontier/.

Porter, M. and M. Kramer. (2011). "Creating Shared Value." *Harvard Business Review*. 89 (1/2).

SABMiller, WWF, and GIZ. (2011). "Water Futures: Addressing Shared Water Challenges through Collective Action." Retrieved from: http://assets.wwf .org.uk/downloads/waterfuturesreportaug2011.pdf.

Sadowski, M. (2013). "The Raters' Response". SustainAbility. Retrieved from: http://sustainability.com/our-work/reports/?topic=ratings.

CHAPTER 3

INVESTIGATING THE SUSTAINABILITY FOOTPRINT OF PATAGONIA

"The most important right we have is the right to be responsible."

—Gerald Amos

This quote is found on the Patagonia website under the section "Becoming a Responsible Company." Although Patagonia is widely recognized to be a leader in sustainability, it remains surprisingly modest about its accomplishments. Founder Yvon Choinard has expressed his reluctance to use the word sustainability. Rather, he prefers the term responsibility.

Patagonia is forthright about the use of resources and the company's efforts to reduce its impact on the environment. It is, after all, in an industry that thrives on selling the latest designs and encouraging consumers to move beyond last year's colors and styles. This is ultimately an unsustainable enterprise. But it can strive to be as responsible as possible. In fact, in late 2018 Patagonia revised its mission statement to a simple statement, "We're in business to save our home planet." They are now all-in on climate change and doing all they can to address the threat of mass extinction (Patagonia n.d.1).

What began as a small company making pitons that essentially destroyed the environment where they were used, today Patagonia is a leader in environmental responsibility. Choinard speaks of starting the Patagonia clothing company as a cash cow, as opposed to the toiling work of the climbing equipment company. With upward of $500 million in sales today, Patagonia has certainly progressed from its days when Choinard was selling climbing gear from the trunk of his car (Choinard and Stanley 2012).

Thinking that clothing from cotton was a natural product, the company had a wakeup call in 1988 when they opened a retail store on Newbury Street in Boston. Within days of the store's opening, employees were complaining of sickness and headaches. After some testing, it was found that the fumes from the dyes and finishing products in the clothes themselves were causing the problem in the tightly sealed environment. Rather than air out the place, the company decided to go to the root of the issue. As Choinard says in his book *The Responsible Company*, "Who knew then that cotton could be as dirty as coal?" (Choinard and Stanley 2012).

Patagonia found that the use of nonorganic cotton was one of the largest impacts in its supply chain due to its intense use of pesticides and herbicides that essentially destroy the soil and everything around the plant except for the cotton fibers themselves. In 1996 it made the move to the exclusive use of organic cotton. Today they also make fleece from recycled plastic bottles and even recycled fleece. The company continues to try to improve its social and environmental impact on the world and has done so with economic benefit (Patagonia n.d.2).

In this chapter we ask you to investigate how Patagonia has improved its own impact on this world by examining and improving its sustainability footprint. How is it tracking and improving its impacts on the environment? How is it improving its social impacts? What effect is this having on its business and how is the company communicating this information to its stakeholders?

Patagonia's website has a tool that allows you to investigate various areas of the world where the company has factories or facilities (http://www.patagonia .com/us/footprint/). It also has a fairly robust resource library describing the various materials it uses for its products and how it chooses those materials (http://www.patagonia.com/materials-tech.html).

Patagonia's "Resource Use" page provides quite a bit of information on water and energy use at the company's facilities and what it has done to minimize its impact in this area (http://www.patagonia.com/resource-use.html). As a private company, it can choose what to disclose, but for our purposes in this chapter, you can see the types of resources it uses and where they might be concentrated.

Later in this book, we will be talking about sustainability reporting and using the Global Reporting Initiative (GRI) standards. Patagonia publishes information on sustainability in a number of ways, but it does not publish according to GRI standards. On its website FAQ page, the company states that it recognizes the value of reporting along the GRI framework as this allows for comparison to other companies, but Patagonia also states that it prefers a more creative and interactive form of reporting and hence has not yet elected to use the GRI standard. You should take a look at the FAQ page; it contains some interesting questions and comments regarding the company's approach (http://www.patagonia .com/corporate-responsibility-faqs.html).

In 2012 Patagonia became the first company in California to register as a B-Corp, or benefit corporation. B-Corp status allows companies to legally protect their missions and visions and to prevent another company from changing these values through acquisition (B Lab 2016). Patagonia states in its B-Corp annual report that this status allows the company to "codify their values" and ensure it can continue to serve the environmental and social causes it holds dear. This makes these values an integral part of its business (Patagonia 2013).

I have provided a number of links to reports and other information regarding Patagonia at the end of this chapter. Take a look at those that interest you, and delve into one of the upcoming questions to investigate this interesting and groundbreaking company.

ADDITIONAL RESOURCES

The Global Environmental Management Initiative (GEMI) is a nonprofit organization that promotes leadership in sustainability for businesses. They have published a number of white papers. This is a rather comprehensive document, but like others you will see in your studies of this topic, it could be a useful tool for your future sustainability practice:

- GEMI value chain: http://gemi.org/supplychain/resources/ForgingNew Links.pdf.
- GEMI has also developed an interactive supply chain tool: http://gemi .org/gemisupplychainsustainabilitytool/.

This is an older document (from 1995), but it is a good overall summary of what a life-cycle assessment involves—"Note on Life-Cycle Analysis," University of Michigan:

- http://www.umich.edu/~nppcpub/resources/compendia/CORPpdfs/ CORPlca.pdf.

The website of *thinkstep* offers a variety of resources and white papers on life-cycle analysis (LCA):

- https://www.thinkstep.com/life-cycle-assessment-lca-methodology.

"Leadership in the Age of Transparency." *Harvard Business Review.* (2010)— this article delves into the externalities often ignored by businesses and stresses the importance of transparency regarding a company's corporate footprint:

- https://hbr.org/product/leadership-in-the-age-of-transparency/R1004A -PDF-ENG.

ADDITIONAL RESOURCES FOR THIS CASE

Suggested additional reading on Patagonia includes the following:

- Patagonia Footprint Chronicles: http://www.patagonia.com/footprint.html.
- Patagonia Reference Library for Footprint: http://www.patagonia.com/reference-library.html.

The Walmart Sustainability Assessment—also known as the Walmart 15 Questions—was published in 2009 and shook up the sustainability community:

- Walmart Supplier Sustainability Assessment: https://grist.files.wordpress.com/2011/11/4055.pdf.

Walmart has since published a new format in conjunction with one hundred various product categories:

- https://corporate.walmart.com/global-responsibility/environment-sustainability/sustainability-index-leaders-shop.
- Information on sustainable cotton at Cotton Connect: http://cottonconnect.org/why-sustainable-cotton/.

AND THERE'S MORE! LINKS TO THE INTERNATIONAL ORGANIZATION FOR STANDARDIZATION (ISO) INFORMATION

ISO provides various frameworks to help an organization achieve sustainable practices, and they are available for purchase through ISO. Here are some links to summaries and more information about ISO:

- Overview of ISO 50001 Energy Management: https://www.iso.org/iso-50001-energy-management.html.
- Overview of ISO 14040 Environmental Management—Life-cycle Assessment—Principles and Framework: https://www.iso.org/standard/37456.html.

QUESTIONS FOR THIS CHAPTER

1. *Boundaries*: What types of boundaries is Patagonia setting in its footprint chronicles? There are suppliers and factories located all over the world, as you can see, but how far into each of these processes is it

looking? Pick one of the processes, such as a textile plant or an assembly plant, and determine the scope of its investigation into the particular footprint. Is the company just looking at environmental or social concerns? How are the economic impacts considered when making decisions? Is the mission of the company driving the decision or are other factors being considered?

2. *Priorities*: How is Patagonia prioritizing its various efforts in its sustainability footprint? Can you find a pattern or framework for the areas it is investigating? Are groups of employees participating in the decisions or is it coming from management? Are suppliers involved in the decisions as well?

3. *Analysis*: What tools are being used at Patagonia to analyze the data of the various footprint concerns? Is it using process mapping, LCA, or value-chain analysis? Can you find any evidence of a balanced scorecard being used? Delve into one of the sustainability footprint areas and see if you can determine how it is analyzing the data and making decisions based upon that analysis.

4. *Business case*: How has Patagonia developed a business case for its sustainability efforts? Can you find evidence of where it has wrestled with any added expense and justified the investments? What kinds of planning has it done to incorporate the sustainability efforts into its overall business plans? How would you classify Patagonia according to the most recent MIT/BCG surveys from Chapter 1 and what evidence would you use to support that classification?

5. *Climate change*: What specifically is Patagonia doing to reduce its footprint in relation to climate change? Are they doing more than reducing their energy use and energy sources? How are they influencing others to join their efforts? How has their sustainability footprint changed in relation to their carbon footprint?

REFERENCES

B Lab. (2016). "Why Is Benefit Corp Right for Me?" Retrieved from: http://benefitcorp.net/businesses/why-become-benefit-corp.

Choinard, Y. and V. Stanley. (2012). *The Responsible Company: What We've Learned from Patagonia's First 40 Years*. Ventura, CA: Patagonia Books.

Jana, R. (2012). "Patagonia's Sales Rise, Thanks to Buyers It Doesn't Design For." SmartPlanet. Retrieved from: http://www.smartplanet.com/blog/decoding-design/patagonias-sales-rise-thanks-to-buyers-it-doesnt-design-for/.

Patagonia. (n.d.1). "Patagonia's Mission Statement." Retrieved March 3, 2019 from: https://www.patagonia.com/company-info.html.

Patagonia. (n.d.2). "Becoming a Responsible Company." Retrieved September 5, 2016 from: http://www.patagonia.com/responsible-company.html.

Patagonia. (2013). "Annual Benefit Corporation Report: Fiscal Year 2013." Retrieved from: http://www.patagonia.com/on/demandware.static/Sites-patagonia-us -Site/Library-Sites-PatagoniaShared/en_US/PDF-US/bcorp_annual_report _2014.pdf.

CHAPTER 4

CISCO SYSTEMS: LEADER IN GOVERNANCE AND ETHICS

A key part of the business model for many leading companies today is creating business value using sustainability. In this chapter we will investigate how governance philosophies and structures are significant drivers of sustainability in an organization.

How have some of the leading companies benefited from strong governance policies and practices? It can be more than just promoting ethical behavior or preventing corruption. You will see as you investigate this issue, good governance can be applied throughout the company's processes to improve productivity and reliability.

In this chapter we will focus upon Cisco Systems. Headquartered in San Jose, CA, and with offices worldwide, Cisco develops, manufactures, and sells networking hardware, telecommunications equipment, and other high-technology services and products. It employs over 74,000 people located in 400 offices and in 2018 its revenues topped $49 billion (Cisco Systems 2018).

Cisco is widely recognized for its responsible behavior, and it has received numerous awards of excellence for governance. The Ethisphere Institute has recognized Cisco as one of the World's Most Ethical Companies from 2008 to 2016. Appendix 4.2 provides more information about the Ethisphere's methodology and its recent changes. In the words of Mark Chandler, Cisco senior vice president and chief compliance officer, "A commitment to ethical conduct—and to the governance structures that ensure we walk the talk—provides the foundation for us to earn our stakeholders' trust. We are focused on addressing concerns around high-priority issues such as digital rights, ethical conduct, and data security and privacy" (Cisco Systems 2015).

What can we learn from Cisco's governance policies and practices? One way to look more critically at Cisco's performance in this area is to compare them with those of another company. Later in this book we will be focusing on Unilever. Unilever is widely recognized for its sustainability practices, especially in the social responsibility arena. Ethisphere selected Unilever as an awardee in

2009, but it has since fallen off that list. You might consider comparing Cisco with Unilever to try to understand the difference between the two companies and see if you can determine why Cisco is seen as a leader in this area and why Unilever, although widely respected in a number of sustainability areas, does not merit top billing for governance from Ethisphere's perspective. It is also interesting to consider why Cisco was left off the Ethisphere list in 2017–2019. Ethisphere changed their methodology in 2017 to include an increase in emphasis on board and executive diversity. This may be one of the reasons Cisco did not make the cut in recent years. Its 2019 board includes only two women and virtually no racial diversity. Senior management has a similar ratio, although it is a bit more diverse. This may be an area that Cisco needs to address to improve its governance overall (Cisco Systems 2019).

GUIDELINES FOR BUSINESS CONDUCT

A fundamental element in making the business case for sustainability is to develop a governance structure that will reinforce its stated goals and allow the company to realize the business value that it has promised. The United Nations Environmental Programme (UNEP) Finance Initiative (UNEP FI) and World Business Council for Sustainable Development (WBCSD) together published an excellent report that provides guidelines to drive this process. Entitled "Translating ESG into Sustainable Business Value," this report's tools are based on surveys with a number of companies with strong ESG (environmental, social, and governance) practices. Successfully communicating ESG factors to stakeholders, including investors, can be an important step in reinforcing the business value of sustainability (WBCSD and UNEP FI 2010).

Materiality is an important concept for analysis in sustainability circles, and we will be investigating materiality throughout this book. The UNEP document discusses the difference in perspective between investors and companies regarding materiality of information. What may seem to be important to a company internally may be unimportant to investors and vice versa (WBCSD and UNEP FI 2010). A link to this document is provided at the end of this chapter. In Annex A of the report, the key performance indicators (KPIs) for good governance are as follows (WBCSD and UNEP FI 2010):

- Codes of conduct and business principles
- Accountability
- Transparency and disclosure
- Implementation—quality and consistency

Table 4.1 shows the detail of the quantitative and qualitative data suggested for each of these KPIs.

Table 4.1 KPIs for good governance (WBCSD and UNEP FI 2010)

KPI	'G' factor	Quantitative Data	Qualitative Data
Governance (From WBCSD Beyond Reporting 2006)	Codes of conduct and business principles	• Number of sustainability initiatives and networks where the company is an active signatory or member	• How does your business model provide value to society? • What core business decisions and new market opportunities have been driven by your understanding of material sustainability issues? • What drives value in your business and what sustainability issues are central to those drivers?
	Accountability	• Number of independent directors on the Board	• How are corporate functions and management and employee incentives aligned to value drivers and understanding of material sustainability issues? • What processes are in place to work with stakeholders according to key accountabilities? • Based on drivers of value, what is the company accountable for and who is the company accountable to?
	Transparency and disclosure	• Number of legal disputes against company filed • Fees paid for litigation costs • Remuneration of senior management and board members in absolute terms; and relative to national, regional, sector, and company (internal) average	• What policies does your company have to communicate market sensitive information to investors as soon as it arises? • What policies do you have to prevent bribery and corruption within your company? • How does your proposed M&A activity affect your company's corporate disclosure obligations?
	Implementation—quality and consistency	• Code of conduct	• Is your company's code of conduct consistently implemented? Is it biting (reinforcing good practice)? Is there evidence that the code of conduct contributes to overall performance?

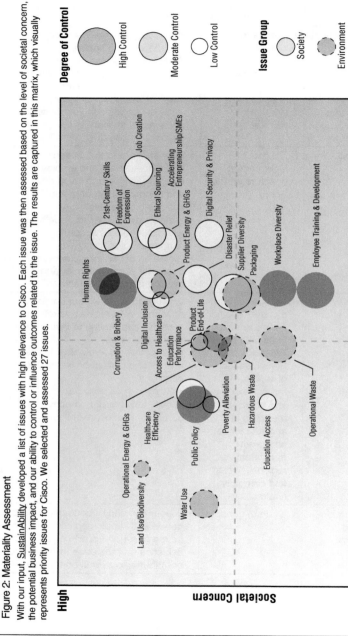

Figure 2: Materiality Assessment
With our input, SustainAbility developed a list of issues with high relevance to Cisco. Each issue was then assessed based on the level of societal concern, the potential business impact, and our ability to control or influence outcomes related to the issue. The results are captured in this matrix, which visually represents priority issues for Cisco. We selected and assessed 27 issues.

Figure 4.1   Cisco materiality assessment (Courtesy of Cisco Systems, Inc. (2013) Unauthorized use not permitted)

As you can see from reading the details in Table 4.1, the statements are not prescriptive. Rather, the data requested and questions asked provoke a self-analysis and an opportunity for a company to set its own goals for improvement. Instead of dictating certain policies, it asks about what policies are in place to promote responsible behavior. And it asks the company to determine how it is addressing key material issues in these various areas.

Cisco also refers to materiality in the governance section of its corporate sustainability report. Cisco worked with SustainAbility to develop key issues of various stakeholders that were prioritized according to relevance and societal concern (see Figure 4.1).

In Figure 4.1, the elements in the upper-right quadrant would be the most material for Cisco to focus on. They represent those in the higher area of emphasis for both impact and societal concern.

Using the materiality analysis—selecting the appropriate issues to focus on—helps a company like Cisco manage risk and develop resiliency in its business without wasting valuable resources on issues that may have a low priority for its most important stakeholders. Good governance policies promote this kind of important planning and analysis.

In the governance section of Cisco's 2015 Corporate Social Responsibility (CSR) report, the company follows up on the materiality analysis from the previous years and outlines some of the key issues it will focus on in the near term. Figure 4.2 shows Cisco's highest priorities for the next year.

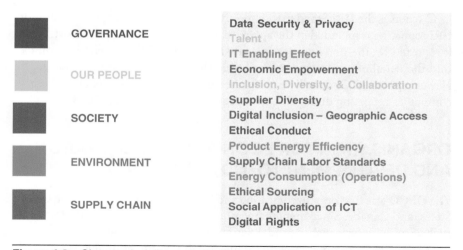

Figure 4.2   Cisco materiality analysis (Courtesy of Cisco Systems, Inc. (2015) Unauthorized use not permitted)

The follow-up of Cisco's reporting on its materiality and connecting the dots between three years of CSR reporting with materiality as a focus shows part of the maturity of Cisco's governance. The company is taking sustainability seriously by engaging with various stakeholder groups to determine the most important issues, both from its own perspective and from those of their various important stakeholders. We will investigate stakeholder engagement more closely in the next chapter, but for now, it is helpful to recognize the importance of looking beyond the walls of the company and the parameters of internal financial statements.

THE GLOBAL REPORTING INITIATIVE (GRI)

Reporting is an important part of the governance of a company, especially as it relates to transparency. In this regard, the Global Reporting Initiative has become a leading framework for reporting on sustainability for multinational corporations. The most recent version of the GRI Standards emphasizes the importance of materiality. In previous versions, materiality was a factor, but the way the reporting system was designed, a higher grade could be acquired by reporting on more items. There was some criticism that companies were gaming the system by reporting on every possible area and hence receiving an *A* for self-reporting. The new standards are constructed differently and they help to prevent this type of activity. A link to the full GRI Standards is posted at the end of this chapter.

Cisco uses the GRI Standards to report on its sustainability performance. Its GRI reporting is included in the appendix section of its 2015 CSR report, where it reported on the previous version of GRI and the GRI Guidelines—you can find the detail of its governance reporting there as well (Cisco Systems 2015). Newer reports for Cisco will be performed under the GRI Guidelines, which all companies reporting under GRI were required to use as of July 2018.

ORGANISATION FOR ECONOMIC CO-OPERATION AND DEVELOPMENT (OECD) GUIDELINES

The OECD was first organized in 1960 and included most of Europe, the United States, and Canada. Since then, many other developed countries have joined its ranks, and it has established guidelines for multinational companies to encourage sustainable economic growth, financial stability, and equitable world trade practices. These guidelines provide recommendations to encourage compliance with local laws and regulations, transparent stakeholder engagement, and responsible business conduct.

The OECD has recognized the importance of strong corporate governance principles toward its goal of improving investor confidence and economic efficiency. This could also be interpreted as a positive business case for good governance in any company. Appropriate governance and planning inherently provide the tools for stakeholder engagement and effective monitoring of procedures. This results in greater efficiency and productivity, resulting in a lower cost of capital (OECD 2004).

The OECD Guidelines were previously updated in 2004, and their newest version, published in September 2015, is now available. A link to this version is provided at the end of this chapter.

ADDITIONAL RESOURCES

There are many tools and guidelines to choose from in the governance area. The following are some to investigate as you work through the questions on this case:

- *Governance excerpts from the earlier GRI*—The GRI has become a leading framework for reporting and is now moving into certification of its reporting framework as a standard. Here is a link to its online section on governance reporting from the earlier G4 version: https://g4.global reporting.org/general-standard-disclosures/governance-and-ethics/ governance/Pages/default.aspx.
- *The Governance of Corporate Responsibility, the Doughty Centre*—The Doughty Centre is associated with the Cranfield School of Management in the United Kingdom. It works with businesses and partners with other organizations to promote and publish the latest innovations in corporate responsibility: http://www.som.cranfield.ac.uk/som/p15144/ Knowledge-Interchange/Guides/Corporate-Responsibility-and-Sustain ability/The-Governance-of-Corporate-Responsibility-Doughty-Centre -How-To-Guide.
- *ISO 26000 Social Responsibility Standard*—The ISO standards are only available for purchase, but there are previews available on the ISO website: https://www.iso.org/obp/ui/#iso:std:iso:26000:ed-1:v1:en.
- *Sarbanes-Oxley overview*—The Sarbanes-Oxley Act was passed in 2002, partly in reaction to the Enron scandal, and has had a big impact on corporate governance. You can read a summary of it at: http://www .sarbanes-oxley-101.com/sarbanes-oxley-compliance.htm.

- *UNEP Report: Translating ESG into Sustainable Business Value*—The World Business Council for Sustainable Development and the United Nations Environment Programme Finance Initiative jointly published this guide to aid businesses in realizing the business case for sustainability. This document was the result of global workshops conducted among businesses, investors, and other stakeholders: http://www.unepfi.org/fileadmin/documents/translatingESG.pdf.
- *OECD Principles of Corporate Governance*—The OECD was founded in 1960 and its membership now includes many of the world's developed countries. Its mission is to promote policies that improve the economic and social well-being of people around the world, and it works with business and labor representatives to encourage better business practices. Here is a link to its principles published in 2015: https://www.oecd.org/daf/ca/Corporate-Governance-Principles-ENG.pdf.
- United Nations Global Impact Corporate Governance Brochure—This is a concise overview of the importance of good governance practices based on the OECD principles: https://www.ifc.org/wps/wcm/connect/a2b5ef8048a7e2db96cfd76060ad5911/IFC_UNGC_brochure.pdf?MOD=AJPERES.

ADDITIONAL CASE RESOURCES

Cisco has developed an interactive Code of Business Conduct available on its website. This tool has user-friendly icons encouraging investigation and direct links to reporting important issues:

- https://investor.cisco.com/investor-relations/governance/code-of-conduct/default.aspx.

Cisco's controller, Jeremy Wilson, former compliance officer at Cisco, was interviewed by Ethisphere in 2013. He mentioned that Cisco was developing internal software to make it easier to report on conflicts of interest as well as entertainment and gifts. This is a creative way to facilitate communication amid a business whose business is communication (Admin 2013). You may wish to read Jeremy Wilson's full comments on the Ethisphere online magazine, including other quotes from the 2012 World's Most Ethical Companies winners:

- https://insights.ethisphere.com/highlights-of-select-winners-from-the-2012-worlds-most-ethical-companies/.

I encourage you to investigate various areas of Cisco and Unilever governance policies and procedures. You will have an opportunity to examine how a leader in this area is using the various tools and standards that are available to improve business operations. Links to Cisco and Unilever reporting:

- Link to current Cisco reports: https://www.cisco.com/c/en/us/about/csr/csr-report.html.
- Link to Cisco Code of Business Conduct: https://investor.cisco.com/investor-relations/governance/code-of-conduct/default.aspx.

Link to Cisco Governance:

- Link to Unilever Code of Business Principles: https://www.unilever.com/Images/code-of-business-principles-and-code-policies_tcm244-409220_en.pdf.
- Link to Unilever Governance: https://www.unilever.com/investor-relations/agm-and-corporate-governance/our-corporate-governance/.
- Link to Ethisphere Scoring and Methodology: https://ethisphere.com/what-we-do/eq-and-benchmarking/.

QUESTIONS FOR THIS CHAPTER

1. *Foundation/Roadmap*: How has Cisco developed a roadmap and foundation for its governance policies? Can you find evidence of the company using international guidelines or frameworks to help it develop its guidelines? Its CSR report states that collaboration is an important part of the company's planning process. Can you determine who its collaborators are and what the benefits are? What challenges has Cisco faced in this journey, and how has it met those challenges? What is the business case for Cisco to develop strong governance policies?

2. *Code of Conduct/Mission*: Take a look at the Code of Business Conduct for Cisco and its mission and core values. Do they seem consistent? How do they compare with those of other multinational companies such as Unilever? If you are investigating another case company or the company you work for, how do these documents compare with those of your company?

3. *Transparency/Accountability*: How transparent is Cisco compared to other companies? What role does governance play in this regard? Who appears to be leading the way in disclosure of information? Is it risky to be more transparent, or does that actually reduce risk? Can you find

information to back up your opinions in this regard? How does Cisco manage risk through its governance processes? Does it follow any international standards or use the help of other institutions such as the WBCSD or UNEP?

4. *Implementation and Engagement*: How does Cisco engage with its stakeholders? Does it employ different methods than other companies such as Unilever? If so, which methods do you think are more effective? How does it affect Cisco's market value?

REFERENCES

Admin. (2013). "Highlights of Select Winners from the 2012 World's Most Ethical Companies." Ethisphere. Retrieved from: https://insights.ethisphere.com/highlights-of-select-winners-from-the-2012-worlds-most-ethical-companies/.

Cisco Systems. (2013). "2013 Corporate Social Responsibility Report; Governance & Ethics." San Jose, CA: Cisco Systems, Inc. Retrieved March 31, 2019 from: https://www.cisco.com/assets/csr/pdf/CSR_Report_2013.pdf#page=11.

Cisco Systems. (2015). "2015 Corporate Social Responsibility Report." San Jose, CA: Cisco Systems, Inc. Retrieved March 31, 2019 from: https://www.cisco.com/assets/csr/pdf/CSR_Report_2015.pdf.

Cisco Systems. (2018). "Cisco Systems, Inc. 2018 Annual Report." San Jose, CA: Cisco Systems, Inc. Retrieved June 27, 2019 from: https://www.cisco.com/c/dam/en_us/about/annual-report/2018-annual-report-full.pdf.

Cisco Systems. (2019). Executive Officers. Retrieved June 28, 2019 from: https://investor.cisco.com/corporate-governance/executive-officers/default.aspx.

OECD. (2004). "OECD Principles of Corporate Governance." Paris, France: OECD. Retrieved from: http://www.oecd.org/corporate/ca/corporategovernanceprinciples/31557724.pdf.

World Business Council for Sustainable Development (WBCSD) and United Nations Environment Programme Financial Initiative (UNEP FI). (2010). "Translating ESG into Sustainable Business Value, Key Insights for Companies and Investors." Geneva, Switzerland: WBCSD and UNEP FI.

CHAPTER 5

ENGAGING STAKEHOLDERS: LEVI STRAUSS & CO.

In this case we will investigate the value of stakeholder engagement for corporations. Many companies have realized its importance, but especially for apparel companies, it has become apparent that stakeholder engagement is paramount to controlling issues in their supply chains.

A leading manufacturer of apparel, Levi Strauss & Co. is ranked number 542 in the Fortune global list for 2017 (Fortune 2017). The *inventor* of jeans, it also manufactures casual wear and other accessories for men and women under the brands of Levi, Dockers, Signature for Levi Strauss & Co., and Denizen. The company emphasizes strong values and sustainable practices on the front page of its website and states that it strives to embed sustainability into every part of its business. Levi Strauss has been widely recognized for its sustainability efforts, ranking first in the jeans category for both Treehugger and GoodGuide (LS&Co. 2016a; LS&Co. 2016b).

Levi Strauss was one of the first to adopt a strong code of conduct—or Terms of Engagement (TOE)—for its suppliers in the early 1990s and relied on that to set labor standards, health and safety measures, and environmental controls. But Levi Strauss, Gap, and other U.S. manufacturers got a wake-up call in 1999 when they were sued over inferior labor conditions in the South Pacific. The suit was settled for $20 million, part of which was used to establish a program to monitor labor conditions and promote change (Smith, Ansett, and Erez 2011).

There had been other flare-ups with labor issues in Southeast Asia, but this lawsuit was terrible publicity for these companies and it was a turning point for Levi Strauss and others. Many had created codes of conduct for their suppliers in the early 1990s, hoping to defray the kinds of practices that were brought to light in the suit. They focused on compliance with standards in health, safety, and environmental requirements that were based on such internationally recognized guidelines as the International Labor Organization (ILO) and the core conventions of the UN Universal Declaration of Human Rights (UN UDHR) (Ceres and Levi Strauss & Co. 2012). Why didn't these codes of conduct work? Suppliers' signatures were on the documents and audits were conducted, but this did not seem to resolve the issues of unfair labor practices.

In 2011 Levi Strauss realized that it wasn't going far enough to get the results it wanted with the TOE approach. The company wanted to go beyond compliance and find real value in its supply chain by incentivizing suppliers to do better in areas of efficiency, productivity, and workers' benefits. It also needed to reduce the risk of factories that appeared to be passing audits but, in fact, were out of compliance. How to resolve this? The company realized it needed to engage with its suppliers and other interested parties and to collaborate with them to find innovative solutions. This was partly the right thing to do, as many businesses say, but it was also a way to find more value by improving reliability, productivity, and overall resiliency of the company.

To do this, it developed a two-step process. First, the company hired Business for Social Responsibility (BSR) to work with its suppliers to develop local, specialized programs that fit the specific needs of those suppliers. Then it partnered with Ceres, a leading sustainability nongovernmental organization (NGO), to develop a robust stakeholder engagement process and prioritize goals to improve the sustainability of its supply chain overall and to exceed compliance with its code of conduct.

After the program was developed, it started with some pilot projects to make sure the plans would work with various suppliers. The goal was to provide what workers really want and care about instead of what Levi Strauss thought they cared about. The company also needed to listen to the factory owners to be able to find a program that would work for them and that they could commit to with enthusiasm rather than by force. As David Lowe, head of supply chain sustainability at Levi Strauss, has stated, this was not a one-size-fits-all program. Rather, it was structured to provide flexibility for various suppliers in different situations and to be able to adapt to changing circumstances and needs (Ceres and Levi Strauss & Co. 2012).

Levi Strauss worked with many partners in its project with Ceres, including retailers H&M and Marks & Spencer, the AFLCIO, other suppliers, NGOs such as Oxfam and the Environmental Justice Foundation, and even other industry leaders in sustainability such as Hewlett Packard. By engaging in dialogues with these organizations, Levi Strauss was able to receive valuable feedback on its strategy and vision for a more sustainable supply chain. It first agreed upon an inclusive approach to collecting information, guided by the principles (Ceres and Levi Strauss & Co. 2012) that follow.

THE GUIDING PRINCIPLES

1. Listen to workers' voices to remain relevant and responsive;
2. Prioritize strategic suppliers that operate in countries with the greatest need;
3. Invest in programs with demonstrated impact, but be willing to pilot initiatives to address unmet needs;
4. Concentrate on factory-level efforts that can also impact workers' families and communities;
5. Track progress by using metrics and qualitative tools to capture impact;
6. Leverage scale, impact, and LS&Co.'s leadership in the industry by partnering with global, national, and local stakeholders; and
7. Share lessons and successes to inspire others to improve workers' well-being.

Moreover, the stakeholders emphasized that there must be an overall commitment to workers' rights as a foundation of this program. It must be self-sustaining; that is, they should be flexible, and local partners need to be established to ensure that the programs don't lose support over time. Workers also need to be involved in the planning to ensure that they are relevant to each area's needs. Metrics need to be established to provide meaningful assessment. Finally, local public policy needs to be considered to ensure that regulations do not conflict with or prohibit progress in a certain area (Ceres and Levi Strauss & Co. 2012).

Overall, the company developed a focused strategy based on the Millennium Development Goals. It decided to concentrate on five major areas (Ceres and Strauss & Co. 2012):

- Economic empowerment
  - *Goal*: workers and their families are enabled to raise their standard of living. Workers, their families, and communities gain sufficient knowledge and access to services to manage their finances.
- Good health and family well-being
  - *Goal*: workers, their families, and communities are enabled to understand, identify, acquire, and apply necessary health resources and practices.
- Equality and acceptance
  - *Goal*: workers are protected from harassment and discrimination. Workers' voices are recognized and respected, and workers are able to freely communicate and dialogue with management. Communication skills are extended to household and community members.

- Education and professional development
  - ◻ *Goal*: workers and their families—and, where possible, communities—are provided access to basic education (reading and writing) and an opportunity to develop other professional development skills.
- Access to a safe and healthy environment
  - ◻ *Goal*: workers, their families, and communities have access to clean water; sanitation; a safe, clean living environment; and community infrastructure.

In each area, the company selected particular items to focus on and metrics to measure progress, as well as overarching recommendations for improvement. The foundation of the program is to protect workers' rights and to develop partnerships within the local communities to facilitate these goals.

As part of this plan and process, in late 2014 Levi Strauss entered into a partnership with IFC, the World Bank's International Finance Corporation, to encourage its suppliers to be more responsible with workers' rights and to follow Levi's TOE. To encourage better audit scores and to reinforce its efforts to improve workers' conditions with a carrot rather than a stick, Levi Strauss has developed a program of short-term financing to small and medium suppliers for environmentally and socially related improvements. Those with higher scores from Levi's auditing evaluations will receive lower interest rates as compensation.

The program is being rolled out gradually, beginning with pilot initiatives in Southeast Asia, where they have faced challenges with suppliers in the past. So far, all of Levi's suppliers in Pakistan and Bangladesh appear to be interested in the program. Financing for these companies is traditionally difficult to find, so the offer of capital at reduced rates could be a win for both the company and its suppliers. Such an influx of funds can improve workers' conditions and productivity as well. Hopefully, this will soon continue to countries like Cambodia, where Levi Strauss has struggled to improve wages and supplier conduct (Mirmotahari 2014; Kourabas 2015).

Levi Strauss has links on its website to its other pilot programs in workers' rights and case studies, surveys, and white papers regarding workers in various countries. The company claims that its suppliers are seeing a return of three dollars for every one dollar invested in the program, and so it is planning to continue to expand its TOE programs to more suppliers in its supply chain (LS&Co. 2016c).

You will find in your investigations for this case, and in future cases where we delve more deeply into supply chain issues, that these are not easy problems to solve. Cultural norms, unstable governments, access to capital, and corruption can undermine the best of intentions from a company and its codes of conduct. Encouraging compliance and improvement can be a winding path and not always a path to success. Partnering with NGOs and local organizations can help, and it takes perseverance, teamwork, and creativity to find solutions.

OTHER PARTNERS

Besides the NGOs mentioned so far, there are a number of international organizations available to multinational corporations, both for networking and guidance. Levi Strauss is a strong supporter of the United Nations Global Compact (UNGC), whose ten principles on environment, society, and anti-corruption are widely respected. In 2015 the UNGC unveiled its updated 17 Sustainable Development goals aimed "to end extreme poverty, fight inequality and injustice, and protect our planet" (UNGC n.d.). Besides the UNGC, there are similar programs at the World Bank, including the International Finance Corporation program mentioned above (IFC 2016), and the Organization for Economic Cooperation and Development (OECD 2016). These programs address the three responsibilities of sustainability over a broad range of countries and cultures.

I have included the two volumes of AccountAbility's Stakeholder Engagement Guides in the supplementary reading recommendations for this case, and Volume 2 is particularly helpful. Although it is a bit intimidating at first because of its length, there are forms and tools that can actually help to map out the most important stakeholders to consider, and there are suggestions on how to engage with them. This can help to avoid dangerous pitfalls. See if you can find comparisons between the AccountAbility Guidelines and the steps that Levi Strauss took in its stakeholder engagement process.

Since it is difficult to keep up with all the stakeholder interests that are funneled through NGOs, it is prudent for a company to be active with industry associations that serve to look out for issues and help engage those stakeholder groups with a broad range of industry support. Levi Strauss mentions a number of partners and collaborators on its website and notes the importance of working with governments as well as various NGOs to promote its commitment to values and sustainability (LS&Co. 2016d).

I invite you to investigate the stakeholder engagement partnership spearheaded by Levi Strauss and its various partners in this case study and to analyze its progress through the case study reports and other information provided by this exemplar in sustainability.

ADDITIONAL RESOURCES

AccountAbility is a think tank headquartered in London but with offices around the world. Its stakeholder engagement standard provides a framework for companies to formulate a successful stakeholder engagement program:

- AA1000: AccountAbility Stakeholder Engagement Standard: http://www.accountability.org/standards/.

SustainAbility is an NGO founded in 1987 with a deep history of engagement with companies to improve social and environmental responsibility. These two manuals are comprehensive—they are something to keep for your toolkit for future reference in planning and implementing a stakeholder engagement program. They contain many tools and tables to help organize your thinking and your approach.

- Stakeholder Engagement Manual, Vol. 1: Guide to Practitioner's Perspectives: http://www.mas-business.com/docs/Vol%201%20Stakeholder%20 Engagement%20Practitioners%20Perspectives.pdf.
- Stakeholder Engagement Manual, Vol. 2: Practitioner's Handbook: http://www.unep.fr/shared/publications/pdf/WEBx0115xPA-SEhand bookEN.pdf.

ADDITIONAL CASE RESOURCES

- Link to Levi Strauss Sustainability page: http://www.levistrauss.com/sustainability/.

The following link will take you to the joint report from 2012 that was mentioned in the case, outlining the strategy for Levi Strauss to improve its stakeholder engagement in the supply chain:

- Ceres-Levi Strauss Report on Stakeholders and Supply Chain: http://www.enterrasolutions.com/media/docs/2012/09/ceres-lsco-whitepaper -2012-04-17.pdf.

A case study of Levi Strauss & Co.'s Supply Chain—this blog post describes the BSR's involvement in Levi's stakeholder engagement process and the setting of goals and metrics:

- Improving Worker Well-Being: https://www.bsr.org/our-insights/blog -view/improving-worker-well-being-a-case-study-of-levi-strauss-cos -supply-chain.

The following website contains a comprehensive code of conduct for suppliers to meet the objectives of Levi Strauss in its supply chain. It is here for your reference to see what this type of document might look like for a large company with a complex supply chain:

- Levi Straus TOE for Suppliers: http://levistrauss.com/wp-content/uploads/ 2017/03/CodeofConduct_English.pdf.

This is a case study published by the *MIT Sloan Management Review* that describes a similar stakeholder engagement process by Gap. You may find it of interest for another perspective on the process:

- "How Gap, Inc. Engaged with Its Stakeholders": https://sloanreview.mit .edu/article/how-gap-inc-engaged-with-its-stakeholders/.

QUESTIONS FOR THIS CHAPTER

1. *Stakeholders*: What were some of the driving forces for Levi Strauss to engage in a stakeholder engagement program for its supply chain? What did this process provide that its TOE weren't providing for the company? How did the process itself work; and how was that different from how Levi Strauss had been operating before? Do you see evidence of the use of any of the tools from the AccountAbility guides in the Levi Strauss process?

2. *Progress*: What has Levi Strauss learned from its pilot programs since it has launched this program in 2011? Is the company noting any changes in policies or procedures for its factories in general, or are they still in the learning phase? (See, for example, the "Worker Rights" page on the Levi Strauss webpage, where you can find various case studies and white papers: https://www.levistrauss.com/how-we-do-business/ worker-well-being/.)

3. *Goals and Metrics*: Dig into the goals and metrics that were established from the stakeholder project. Can you tell how these changed from the previous TOE for Levi Strauss? What shifted and how is that changing the company's approach now? Is Levi Strauss engaged with other companies to make these goals more attainable? What is the business case for this investment of time and energy in the stakeholder engagement program?

4. *Other Partners*: Who are the key international NGOs and business organizations that have been partners with Levi Strauss in its sustainability journey? How have these organizations influenced Levi's stakeholder

engagement program? Do the guidelines encompass most of what the company needs to understand or consider, or does Levi Strauss need to customize the information for each region?

REFERENCES

Ceres and Levi Strauss & Co. (2012). "Improving Workers' Well-Being: A New Approach to Supply Chain Engagement." Retrieved from: http://www .enterrasolutions.com/media/docs/2012/09/ceres-lsco-whitepaper-2012 -04-17.pdf.

Fortune. (2017). "Fortune 500 list." Fortune. Retrieved from: http://fortune .com/fortune500/list/.

IFC. (2016). "About IFC: Overview." Retrieved September 22, 2016, from: https://www.ifc.org/wps/wcm/connect/corp_ext_content/ifc_external _corporate_site/about+ifc_new.

Kourabas, M. (2015). "A Sustainable Supply Chain 'Race to the Top.'" TriplePundit. Retrieved from: https://www.triplepundit.com/special/sustainable -fashion-2014/can-levi-strauss-create-sustainability-race-top-supply-chain/.

LS&Co. (2016a). "Levi Strauss & Co." Retrieved September 22, 2016, from: http://www.levistrauss.com/.

LS&Co. (2016b). "Who We Are: Recognition." Retrieved September 22, 2016, from: http://www.levistrauss.com/who-we-are/recognition/.

LS&Co. (2016c). "Sustainability: People." Retrieved September 22, 2016, from: http://www.levistrauss.com/sustainability/people/#worker-rights.

LS&Co. (2016d). "Who We Are: Our Partners in Progress." Retrieved September 22, 2016, from: http://www.levistrauss.com/who-we-are/#our -partners-in-progress.

Mirmotahari, F. (2014). "Shared Prosperity: IFC and LS&Co. Team Up to Reward Suppliers for Doing the Right Thing." Retrieved from: http://www .levistrauss.com/unzipped-blog/2014/11/05/shared-prosperity-ifc-and -levis-team-up-to-reward-suppliers-for-doing-the-right-thing/.

OECD. (2016). "About the OECD." Retrieved September 22, 2016, from: http:// www.oecd.org/about/.

Smith, N.C., S. Ansett, and L. Erez. (2011). "How Gap Inc. Engaged with Its Stakeholders." *MIT Sloan Management Review*, 52(4). Retrieved from: goo. gl/nKU9XX.

UNGC. (n.d.). "17 Goals to Transform Our World." Retrieved September 20, 2016, from: https://www.unglobalcompact.org/sdgs/17-global-goals.

CHAPTER **6**

ENVIRONMENTAL RESPONSIBILITY: ALCOA CORPORATION

For this chapter focusing on environmental responsibility, it is tempting to choose a company like Interface Carpet or Seventh Generation. But it is more interesting and challenging to provide an example of a resource extraction company or even an oil company—some company in a business that involves developing resources that have pollution issues involved in the processing and extraction of the resource. This is something we, as environmentalists, recoil against, of course. But at the same time, the world has not yet been able to wean itself away from using various natural resources. In fact, some resources—such as rare earth minerals—are utilized in the very industries we use to move away from fossil fuels, for example, powerful magnets used in wind turbines and lasers. So in that light, the goal of this chapter and case is to focus on a resource extraction company that is a leader in its field and sets a higher standard in a difficult industry.

ALCOA AND ENVIRONMENTAL RESPONSIBILITY

Alcoa has a reputation as a leading manufacturer of aluminum products and other lightweight metals. In 2016, Alcoa, Inc. split into two separate companies, Alcoa Corporation and Arconic, Inc., dividing the business between the mining and metal refineries—the upstream company, Alcoa Corp. and the production of parts and materials from these metals—the value-add company, Arconic, Inc. Alcoa Corp. is by far the larger of the two surviving companies, retaining roughly 80 percent of the stock distribution with the other 20 percent going to Arconic (Alcoa 2016a). For our purposes in this chapter, we will focus on Alcoa Corp.

In 2017, Alcoa Corp. had annual revenues of $11.7 billion and employed 14,600 people worldwide, ranking 206 on the Fortune 500 list for 2017. The company was ranked number 151 on the Newsweek Green List for the top 500 companies in the United States in 2017 and was also listed on the Dow Jones Sustainability Index (DJSI). Alcoa's parent company, Alcoa Inc., had been listed as an industry leader on the DJSI for the previous 14 years (Newsweek 2017; Alcoa 2018).

The aluminum industry began in the late 1800s with Charles Martin Hall, who discovered how to produce aluminum by tinkering in his backyard *laboratory* in Ohio. Mr. Hall then joined with a group of investors in Pittsburgh to form the Pittsburgh Reduction Company, and they produced their first commercial ingot of aluminum in 1888. Their initial challenge was to create a market for this newly available metal, and they began by making everyday items like cooking pots and foil, electric wires, and even some of the parts in the engine of the Wright brothers' plane flown at Kitty Hawk. By 1907 their business had grown, and they renamed the company the Aluminum Company of America, later changed to Alcoa, Inc. (Alcoa n.d.).

Today Alcoa manufactures roughly a third of the world's alumina, or aluminum oxide, which is the major ingredient in aluminum. It is refined from bauxite, which is mined and ground into a mix with caustic soda and lime, heated, and washed and dried to form a granular white material similar to table salt. Alcoa's refinery in Australia was the first to be certified to the ISO 9002 quality standard in 1992, followed by two of its other Australian refineries in 1994. In 1997, Alcoa certified its first refinery to the ISO 14001 environmental standard. Since that time, it has certified 63 other locations to this standard (Alcoa 2015b; Alcoa 2016c).

Besides refining bauxite to alumina, Alcoa's major business is smelting aluminum, and it has production facilities worldwide. Think of smelting, and you think of heat. Think of heat, and you think of energy. Alcoa has realized that it can save energy and money by encouraging recycling, both commercially and through everyday consumers. As aluminum is highly recyclable, Alcoa has made a profitable business by using recycled aluminum in the production of much of its aluminum. It takes only one-twentieth the energy to make aluminum from a recycled product versus smelting it from scratch. By engineering its aluminum cans to be 100 percent recyclable, Alcoa can reuse all of that material for new cans, and they can be back on retailer shelves in as little as sixty days (Alcoa 2016b).

The company has a long history of leadership in quality and stewardship. Being in the extraction and refining business, Alcoa faces particular challenges for a company operating in a world of constrained resources and growing population. It is partly for this reason that we chose Alcoa for our case company for this chapter. It would be easier to choose a company that deals mostly with benign resources in our chapter focused on environmental responsibility, but we wanted to give you the opportunity to see the challenges facing a company that works with toxic chemicals and waste products. How can it operate responsibly and set appropriate goals for improving its environmental footprint?

The frameworks and standards developed by ISO can help in this regard; they allow companies to set their own goals and establish a path for continuous improvement. The progress can then be audited and certified. We have provided links at the end of this chapter to ISO 14001 (Environmental Standard) and ISO 50001 (Energy Standard). You may want to spend some time reviewing these standards and considering how they could help a company improve its performance. Alcoa has set goals for both waste and energy improvement. It has met many of its goals, but the company is not shy about admitting where its gaps lie, and it does a pretty good job of reporting its sustainability progress in its annual reports.

Alcoa has organized its business around its core values of integrity, environmental health and safety, innovation, respect, and excellence. Its 2015 sustainability report describes how its governance structure supports its sustainability goals, including the integration of sustainability into its core business strategies. Although its chief sustainability officer (CSO) does not currently sit on the executive council of the company, he does have access to the CEO and other senior officers. In the past, the CSO was part of capital-spending decisions, but it is not clear from the company's current documents whether this is the case. One policy that has continued is that compensation is tied to sustainability, with 20 percent of bonuses tied to meeting sustainability goals across the workforce, including health and safety as well as carbon emissions. The company participates in and is a member of many important organizations that are meant to support its strategic goals, including the Aluminum Stewardship Initiative and the United Nations Global Compact (Alcoa 2015a; Alcoa 2016d).

Another important accomplishment is that Alcoa is the first extraction company to receive cradle-to-cradle certification. It has achieved this certification for most of its upstream and many of its downstream products. It has also performed life-cycle analysis on many of its products (Aster 2014).

Sustainability reporting at Alcoa is taken seriously, and its 2017 report follows the guidelines of the Global Reporting Initiative (GRI). The GRI Standards will be mentioned throughout this book, and in this case you will have a chance to take a look at a report that has been written in accordance with the GRI

Standards, so you can begin to familiarize yourself with its format. In the Alcoa report, you will find the company has performed a materiality analysis to determine the most important aspects to report on based upon its stakeholder input. The eight most material topics listed in its 2017 report are: economic performance, greenhouse gas emissions, energy, water, waste, biodiversity, health and safety, and local communities. There is also an index toward the end organizing the information along the GRI reporting indicators. You will discover that this is a handy tool to find information quickly based on the topic you wish to investigate (Alcoa 2018).

Despite progress in reducing the energy intensity of its products and the waste from its bauxite mining, Alcoa has had some significant challenges. In 2015 it had five separate fatalities at its various facilities, and it also had three fatalities in 2017. Its bauxite mining facilities have improved their residue storage efficiencies, but their residue reuse has fallen short of company goals. This is partially due to the lack of standards in various countries for the use of such products, but the company has managed to produce a market for construction back fill and top turf dressing (Alcoa 2015a; Alcoa 2018). You may find it interesting to investigate some of these issues as you research the questions that are presented for you in this chapter. You may also wish to compare Alcoa against other resource extraction and refining companies such as Teck Resources out of Canada. Teck is highly rated as well and is a smaller company focusing on different minerals, but it is very well respected and is also included in the DJSI (Teck 2016). Overall, this should provide some interesting material to study on this topic.

ADDITIONAL RESOURCES

The following document could be supplemental reading for many of this book's topics, but we are putting it here because it places a strong emphasis on companies that are reducing their energy use and carbon footprint. You were introduced to Ceres's work in the previous chapter about Levi Strauss. Here it focuses more broadly on corporate structure, priorities, and measuring performance, listing 20 key expectations for corporations in the areas of governance, stakeholder engagement, disclosure, and performance. At the end it adds several pages of links to organizations that can provide additional information or support:

- Ceres. (2010). The 21st Century Corporation: The Ceres Roadmap for Sustainability. https://www.ceres.org/resources/reports/21st-century -corporation-ceres-roadmap-sustainability.

This is a follow-up to the previous Ceres document, providing a broad analysis of whether major companies are embracing sustainability and also examples of companies that are excelling in this area. The goal is to inspire more companies to make sustainability a part of the fabric of the company rather than just a group of unconnected green projects. The report is well organized, with summaries and key findings in each area, along with examples of how companies are finding business success by implementing sustainability throughout their corporate structure and supply chains:

- Ceres and Sustainalytics. (2012). The Road to 2020: Corporate Progress on the Road to Sustainability. https://www.ceres.org/resources/reports/road-2020-corporate-progress-ceres-roadmap-sustainability.

For your convenience, here is a link to the environmental compliance disclosures for the GRI Standards:

- GRI implementation—environmental compliance disclosures: https://www.globalreporting.org/standards/media/1014/gri-307-environmental-compliance-2016.pdf.

The ISO 14001 Environmental Management System Standard is the most commonly talked about standard in this family, but you can go to this link and preview the other various standards in the 14000 family. Click on the links under *ISO Store* to preview these standards and their guidelines:

- ISO 14000 Family of Environmental Standards: https://www.iso.org/publication/PUB100238.html.

The following standard is used by companies to improve their energy management performance. The ISO website contains a summary of the standard as well as a preview of some of the free sections of the standard:

- ISO 50001 Energy Management Standard: https://www.iso.org/iso-50001-energy-management.html.

ADDITIONAL CASE RESOURCES

This page has links to the most recent sustainability reports as well as previous reports, the Alcoa Human Rights Policy, and the UN Global Compact Progress Report.

- Alcoa Corp. sustainability webpage: http://www.alcoa.com/sustainability/en/default.asp.

QUESTIONS FOR THIS CHAPTER

1. *Refining Operations*: How has Alcoa addressed its use of materials and resources in its refining operations? For example, how has it reduced its water intensity? What types of tools and standards have helped it improve its performance in this area? Can you decipher how the company has used or could use the ISO 14001 standard or other frameworks to improve its environmental performance? How has Alcoa made a business case for its investments in reducing the footprint of its refining operations?

2. *Mining Operations*: Take a look at the company's bauxite mining operations. How has it performed in this area and what areas are particularly challenging? Can you see how Alcoa has managed to make improvements, and if so, what tools and frameworks have helped it reach its goals? Can you find the key performance indicators for its mining operations and how the company is using this data to drive performance? How does its performance compare with other competitors in the industry?

3. *Energy Efficiency*: What kinds of actions has Alcoa taken to increase its energy efficiency and reduce its carbon footprint? How has Alcoa integrated its energy efficiency improvements into the rest of its sustainability goals? How does this compare with other industry competitors? Is Alcoa implementing ISO 50001 to improve its performance or could you see how it would be helpful? What is the business case for Alcoa's investments in energy improvements?

4. *Ceres*: At the end of this chapter are references to two documents from Ceres related to corporate sustainability and performance. Ceres developed 20 key expectations relating to governance, stakeholder engagement, disclosure, and performance. How would you rate Alcoa in these various areas, especially as it relates to environmental performance? How might the company improve its performance using the Ceres guidelines? How is it including strategies for environmental improvement in its long-term planning for the business overall?

REFERENCES

Alcoa. (2015a). "2015 Alcoa Sustainability Report." Retrieved from: http://www.alcoa.com/sustainability/en/pdfs/2015-Sustainability-Report.pdf.

Alcoa. (2015b). "Unlocking Value: Annual Report 2015." Retrieved from: http://www.alcoa.com/global/en/investment/pdfs/2015_Annual_Report.pdf.

Alcoa. (n.d.). "The Alcoa Story: It All Starts with Dirt." Retrieved September 25, 2016, from: http://www.alcoa.com/global/en/who-we-are/history/default.asp.

Alcoa. (2016a). "Alcoa's Future Value-Add Company to Be Named 'Arconic.'" Retrieved from: http://www.alcoa.com/global/en/news/news_detail.asp?pageID=20160315000324en&newsYear=2016.

Alcoa. (2016b). "Alcoa Expands Recycling Capability—New Expansion Will Increase Recycling Capacity by Nearly 50 Percent." Retrieved from: https://www.alcoa.com/package/en/news/releases/alcoa_expands.asp.

Alcoa. (2016c). "What Is Alumina?" Retrieved September 25, 2016, from: http://www.alcoa.com/alumina/en/info_page/alumina_defined.asp.

Alcoa. (2016d). "Executive Council." Retrieved from: http://www.alcoa.com/global/en/investment/executive_council.asp.

Alcoa. (2018). "2017 Alcoa Sustainability Report." Retrieved from: https://www.alcoa.com/sustainability/en/pdf/2017-Sustainability-Report.pdf.

Aster, N. (2014). Interview, Kevin McKnight, CSO, Alcoa. Retrieved from: http://www. triplepundit.com/2014/05/interview-kevin-mcknight-cso-alcoa/.

Newsweek. (2017). "Green Rankings 2017: U.S. 500." Retrieved from: https://www.newsweek.com/full-list-US-companies-green-rankings-2017-18.

Perera, A. and S. Putt del Pino, (2013). "AkzoNobel and Alcoa Link Sustainability to Capital Projects." GreenBiz.com. Retrieved from: https://www.greenbiz.com/blog/2013/03/21/akzonobel-and-alcoa-link-sustainability-capital-projects.

Teck. (2016). "Teck named to 2016 Dow Jones Sustainability World Index." Retrieved from: http://www.teck.com/news/stories/2016/teck-named-to-2016-dow-jones-sustainability-world-index-.

CHAPTER 7

UNILEVER: LEADER IN SOCIAL RESPONSIBILITY

Unilever's history dates back to the 1890s when William Hesketh Lever, founder of Lever Brothers Company, stated his vision for Sunlight Soap, a product he hoped would revolutionize Victorian England and bring about a new era of cleanliness and hygiene. He hoped "to make cleanliness commonplace; to lessen work for women; to foster health and contribute to personal attractiveness, that life may be more enjoyable and rewarding for the people who use our products" (Unilever 2016a).

Today, Unilever's more than 400 brands are used by over two billion people on any given day, according to the company's website. Its portfolio of products includes Vaseline, Lifebuoy, Lipton, Dove, Hellman's, Suave, Ponds, and even Ben & Jerry's (Unilever 2016b). Yes, it was Unilever who bought Ben & Jerry's in 2000, when it also acquired SlimFast.

It was a match made for commentary. Both were closely held companies at the time, and even though SlimFast was the much larger company, the acquisition of Ben & Jerry's was the one that created a stir, at least in the environmental community. But even though the purchase brought Ben & Jerry's under the umbrella of Unilever, agreements were made that conserved some of the original vision of Ben & Jerry's founders. These included purchasing milk from Vermont dairy farmers at a higher than market rate and donating 7.5 percent of the ice cream company's pretax profit to charity (Branch and Beck 2000).

Unilever is one of the most highly respected companies in the world today, listed at the top by far in the GlobeScan and SustainAbility survey from 2017 (GlobeScan and SustainAbility 2017). It is widely recognized for its leadership in sustainability and its ethical behavior. William Lever's original vision has been expanded, and its corporate purpose now states that the company's success requires "the highest standards of corporate behavior toward everyone we work with, the communities we touch, and the environment on which we have an impact" (Unilever 2016c).

How has Unilever achieved this success? What management tools and systems has it used to facilitate its rise? What organizations and companies has it partnered with to embed its systems throughout its supply chain? How has it made a business case for its investments in local communities and environmental resources? How has it improved its stakeholder engagement? These are some of the questions you can investigate in this chapter as you delve into Unilever's various engagements around the world.

And there is good news for you! Unilever has published extensive information on its website regarding sustainability. There are two smaller overviews of its sustainability plan available for download, and the rest of its information is linked throughout its website. The company's Global Reporting Initiative (GRI) reporting section has a link to a downloadable PDF, Unilever's GRI Index, that contains links to various areas on the website or other documents dealing with specific topics. This helps readers get right to the section they are interested in and also provides an overview of the reporting topics (Unilever 2016d).

This is a relatively new trend in sustainability reporting—allowing the reader to quickly drill down to particular areas of interest rather than having to thumb through pages of sustainability report PDFs, searching for the topic. You will have an opportunity to compare this method of GRI reporting for Unilever versus the more formal sustainability report compiled by Alcoa in the last chapter. Which do you prefer? Advantages of the online system allow for constant updating, but are there also advantages to having everything in one document? It will be interesting to see how companies continue to enhance their reporting and search for the right solution for their particular group of stakeholders.

Unilever's Sustainable Living Plan aims to decouple its growth from its environmental impacts while increasing its positive effects upon society. The company speaks of facing the challenges of climate change while still providing for human development, striving to help people live comfortably while staying within the limits of the natural world and making sustainable living commonplace. To achieve this, Unilever has developed strategies to integrate sustainability into its products and supply chain. It has made public commitments to integrity and good governance and is reporting on its progress at regular intervals (Unilever 2016d). However, Unilever has not achieved all of its goals. Just as other multinational companies struggle with labor issues in their supply chains, so has Unilever. We saw in the chapter on stakeholder engagement how Levi Strauss worked with local NGOs and companies to help resolve its supplier issues. Unilever has also engaged with other organizations, and a 2013 report by Oxfam (Wilshaw et al. 2013) explains some of the issues and challenges in depth regarding labor issues in Vietnam.

Despite codes of conduct and policies prescribed from the top management and audits in the field, problems persist. Oxfam found that the local managers lacked the knowledge and capacity to ensure that the guidelines specified by the company were followed, and Unilever's goals for fair treatment were not met. For example, workers in supplier factories were found to be hired on a temporary basis to avoid the minimum requirements set by Unilever, and overtime hours were well beyond the legal limits. Keeping workers on a temporary basis avoided the right to collective bargaining and other benefits.

Unilever partnered with Oxfam on this report, and it is a testament to the company's commitment to improvement that such transparency was present. Indeed, Unilever's VP of HR for Global Supply Chain recognized the importance of employee welfare when he stated, "Unilever's analysis shows that where there are good conditions and empowerment of employees, the factory has the best results" (Wilshaw et al. 2013). The Oxfam report contains recommendations for proactive stakeholder engagement and management priorities to achieve these goals, as well as a commitment from Unilever to study the problem in depth and implement appropriate procedures to achieve fair working conditions throughout the supply chain.

The current information from Unilever recognizes the continuing challenges of labor rights in countries where laws and governments are not as protective as they are in developed countries. For issues such as child labor, the company is working toward incentivizing its suppliers to do better rather than emphasizing compliance. It is working toward building capacity for its suppliers and promoting and rewarding best practices to encourage more suppliers to perform better rather than competing with one another for low prices (Unilever 2016e). This sounds very similar to what we saw with Levi Strauss's approach.

An updated publication from Oxfam in 2016 reports significant progress from Unilever on many of the labor issues recognized in 2013, but many challenges remain. In particular, the company made progress in Vietnam, increasing trust between workers and managers and improving the grievance procedures. Suppliers are also more aware of expectations, and excessive labor hours have been reduced. However, there are still some key unresolved issues that were addressed in the report: convincing more suppliers of the business case for fair labor treatment, ensuring fair compensation across the board and empowering women, and addressing systemic issues of child labor, slavery, and gender-based violence—issues in the supply chain that affect others besides Unilever (Wilshaw et al. 2016). This is a very tough problem, as you have begun to see, and you will be able to address it from another perspective in this chapter through the lens of Unilever.

I have provided links to various Unilever webpages at the end of this chapter and have also given you a link to the two Oxfam reports. This should give you a start on examining Unilever's activities. You should have an interesting time learning about this company and how it impacts the world's social systems.

ADDITIONAL RESOURCES

- "GRI Standards Introduction." https://www.globalreporting.org/standards/getting-started-with-the-gri-standards/.

Both Oxfam reports refer to the guiding principles as an important reference for Unilever as well as any multinational company. Oxfam highlighted the three pillars of the framework: the government's duty to protect human rights, the company's duty to respect human rights, and the victim's access to remedies. This document provides background and commentary on the development of these principles:

- "UN Guiding Principles on Human Business and Human Rights." https://www.ohchr.org/Documents/Publications/GuidingPrinciplesBusinessHR_EN.pdf.

These guidelines are updated periodically and this most recent version from 2011 has been modified to align with the UNGP. These cover basic ethics for businesses and how to respond to societal expectations as well as obeying international standards:

- "OECD Guidelines for Multinational Enterprises." http://www.oecd.org/corporate/mne/48004323.pdf.

This ISO standard is a guidance standard. That means it cannot be certified, but it is offered to companies for guidance in improving their social responsibility. It can provide a structure and can be coupled with the kind of stakeholder engagement emphasized in the Oxfam reports:

- ISO 26000 Guidance on Social Responsibility. https://www.iso.org/iso-26000-social-responsibility.html.

ADDITIONAL CASE RESOURCES

- "Sustainable Living Plan Report Hub." https://www.unilever.com/sustainable-living/our-sustainable-living-report-hub/.

- "Unilever Human Rights Report." (2015). https://www.unilever.com/Images/unilever-human-rights-report-2015_tcm244-437226_en.pdf.
- Oxfam report. (2013). "Labour Rights in Unilever's Supply Chain: From Compliance Towards Good Practice." https://www.unilever.com/Images/rr-unilever-supply-chain-labour-rights-vietnam-310113-en_tcm244-409769_en.pdf.
- Oxfam report. (2016). "Labour rights in Vietnam: Unilever's Progress and Systemic Challenges." https://www.oxfam.org/en/research/labor-rights-vietnam-unilevers-progress-and-systemic-challenges.
- "Unilever GRI G4 Index." https://www.unilever.com/sustainable-living/our-approach-to-reporting/gri-index/.

QUESTIONS FOR THIS CHAPTER

1. *Social responsibility*: Why has Unilever been recognized as a leader in social responsibility? What types of issues stand out from the perspective of the readings on social responsibility that are provided in this case? How is the company improving its performance? Who are its most important stakeholders and how is Unilever engaging them in this effort? What are some of the challenges the company is facing? Is Unilever transparent about these challenges or do you have to find out about them elsewhere? Can you find the business case for its efforts in improving social impacts?

2. *Sustainable Living Plan*: Take a look at Unilever's Sustainable Living Plan. What are the most material issues from a social responsibility perspective and how has the company selected them? How does improving its performance in these areas affect its performance overall? Is the company cooperating with other organizations or companies to learn about best practices or is Unilever the leader in most cases? Are there differences in various brands or regions or are there universal tools and guidelines used throughout the company?

3. *Oxfam*: Take a look at the Oxfam reports mentioned in this case. What tools and methods does Oxfam recommend to Unilever to improve the labor conditions in its factories in Vietnam? Looking at the second Oxfam report, what kind of progress has Unilever made and how did it accomplish that? What do you think are the toughest challenges and how might those be resolved? Can you find similarities or contrasts with the Levi Strauss stakeholder engagement on this issue?

4. *Standards and performance*: The Oxfam reports also mention international standards and the need for better governance in the countries where Unilever and other major companies operate. How is Unilever using these standards to address the labor challenges it faces in Southeast Asia? Does this help to distinguish Unilever among its peers? How does its strategy and implementation compare with other multinational companies in a similar industry, such as Proctor & Gamble or L'Oreal? How does it compare with companies such as Levi Strauss or Alcoa?

REFERENCES

Branch, S., and E. Beck. (2000). "Unilever Buys Ben & Jerry's, SlimFast for over $2.5 Billion." The Wall Street Journal. Retrieved from: https://www.wsj.com/articles/SB955522850788928066.

GlobeScan and SustainAbility. (2017). "The 2017 Sustainability Leaders; A GlobeScan/SustainAbility Survey." Retrieved from: https://globescan.com/the-2017-gss-sustainability-leaders-report/.

Unilever. (2016a). "Who We Are: Our History." Retrieved October 1, 2016, from: https://www.unilever.com/about/who-we-are/our-history/.

Unilever. (2016b). "Who We Are: About Unilever." Retrieved October 1, 2016, from: https://www.unilever.com/about/who-we-are/about-Unilever/.

Unilever. (2016c). "Who We Are: Purpose, Value and Principles." Retrieved October 1, 2016, from: https://www.unilever.com/about/who-we-are/our-values-and-principles/.

Unilever. (2016d). Introducing Our Plan. Retrieved October 2, 2016, from: https://www.unilever.com/sustainable-living/.

Unilever. (2016e). "Fairness in the Workplace." Retrieved October 2, 2016, from: https://www.unilever.com/sustainable-living/enhancing-livelihoods/fairness-in-the-workplace/.

Wilshaw, R., L. Unger, D.Q. Chi, and P.T. Thuy. (2013). "Labour Rights in Unilever's Supply Chain: From compliance towards good practice; An Oxfam study of Unilever's Vietnam operations and supply chain." Oxfam. Retrieved from: https://www.unilever.com/Images/rr-unilever-supply-chain-labour-rights-vietnam-310113-en_tcm244-409769_en.pdf.

Wilshaw, R., D.Q. Chi, P. Fowler, and P.T. Thuy. (2016). Labour Rights in Vietnam: Unilever's progress and systemic challenges. Oxfam. Retrieved from: https://www.oxfam.org/sites/www.oxfam.org/files/file_attachments/rr-unilever-vietnam-progress-challenges-040716-en.pdf.

CHAPTER 8

ECONOMIC RESPONSIBILITY: ING GROEP NV

Companies successfully engaging in responsible environmental and social practices are more often economically successful as well. Economic success can be one of the results of incorporating environmental and social management systems. Resources are more carefully managed, risks are avoided, employees are more engaged and fulfilled, and data is tracked more carefully. More and more, customers are considering a company's reputation for environmental and social responsibility before purchasing products from that company, and some are even willing to pay a bit more for those products. In addition, a bad reputation in the same vein can drive customers away and send profits downward.

According to a recent study by the Governance & Accountability Institute, companies who are measuring and managing their resources and social responsibilities appear to also perform better in the long term in capital markets. In 2016, 81 percent of S&P companies were reporting on sustainability, up from only 20 percent in 2011. This shows a clear understanding of the importance of strategic planning and managing environmental, social, and governance (ESG) responsibilities for companies. It also indicates a response to shareholder and other stakeholder requests for this type of information (G&A Inst. 2016).

In Chapter 2, links were provided to the *MIT Sloan Management Review* surveys of companies and sustainability practices. The 2013 MIT/BCG survey stated that since 2010, a consistent 35 percent of companies reported that their sustainability efforts contribute directly to profits. A more recent survey from 2016 reported that 60 percent of senior corporate executives said sustainability was materially important to their company's bottom line. Although the query wasn't quite the same, it appears to be an improvement from the 2013 results. In contrast, a remarkable 75 percent of senior investment firm executives stated that sustainability was materially important. This is encouraging news in a way, showing that there is growing pressure from the investment community for businesses to act responsibly (Kiron et al. 2013; Unruh et al. 2016).

It is therefore fitting to choose a case company for economic responsibility that focuses on banking and investments. The financial industry in general is often criticized for focusing on profits at the expense of its customer base and for ignoring climate change and the effects of fossil fuels when considering its investments. With this case you will have an opportunity to compare the performance of a leader in the financial field to its peers from an economic perspective as well as from the perspective of its environmental and social performance.

ING Groep NV has been recognized as a leader in sustainability practices for over a decade, and it has focused on both environmental and social betterment to achieve economic success. The company was rated 54th in the 2018 Corporate Knights Global 100 List of most sustainable companies, and it is also listed as one of the leaders in the banking industry on the Dow Jones Sustainability Index World Index, receiving high ratings for its climate strategy and financial inclusion practices (Corporate Knights 2018; ING 2018e).

Based in the Netherlands, ING operates in 40 countries and employs over 51,000 people. It offers both wholesale and retail banking services to over 37 million people worldwide. With 2017 revenues of over $56 billion, it ranked number 171 in the Fortune Global 500 for 2018 (ING 2018a; Fortune 2018).

ING's sustainability efforts spring from a number of directions, both direct and indirect. Directly, the group is setting and meeting goals to reduce its footprint, from reducing direct emissions to practicing a circular economy. For example, when breaking ground on a headquarters in Amsterdam, ING used the soil from the foundation to make the concrete for the building and for nearby roadways. More broadly, it invests in renewable energy projects and supports clients to achieve their own sustainability goals. The company is also reducing its investment in fossil fuel industries and has a goal to be close to zero for investments in thermal-coal power generation by 2025. Its interest in the circular economy has drawn the company into membership in the CE100 program, an initiative of the Ellen MacArthur Foundation. ING has also financed a number of transactions supporting circular economy-focused companies, like Renewi and Avantium (ING 2018b; 2018c).This type of activity is very refreshing in an industry with a history of conservative, bottom-line-focused policies and entrenchment in the old guard of fossil fuels and carbon-intensive infrastructure investment.

Sustainable financial investment is part of ING's sustainability strategy. Its wholesale banking division seeks to identify a number of clients to support these sustainability goals—those investing in renewable energy, waste management, water, or green buildings; those focusing on resource scarcity; or those with a strong sustainability track record and ambitious agendas for improvement. In 2017 it initiated its first loan that generated a lower interest rate based on the borrower's sustainability performance, and it also issued the first green bond in the United Kingdom for a public utilities project for water. The company is clear about its goals to reduce the impact of climate change, and it aims to encourage other investors to move toward low carbon and renewable options in the energy field (ING 2018c).

ING is truly leading the rest of the financial community in this regard. Only recently have mainstream financial investment companies like Morgan Stanley or Charles Schwab created a sustainability focus, and even then they are mostly concentrated on ESG mutual funds—those that allow customers interested in responsible investment to find a home for their investment dollars. But they are not taking it on with full force as ING has done, incorporating these values across the company and driving investments and customer loans accordingly. Indeed, ING is leading the field and pushing the market in this direction.

ING's sustainability reporting can be found on its website, which has convenient links to various areas of focus. Its annual sustainability reporting summary has been integrated into its overall annual reports since 2015. You will find that this is a growing trend among leaders of the sustainability community, linking the financial results with nonfinancial ones and emphasizing the good business practice of acting responsibly toward the world and its resources.

In spite of the many positives regarding ING's sustainability focus, it has not been flawless in its execution of governance and financial policies. Early in 2018, ING announced in its annual report that it would bring forth a motion to increase the salary of CEO Ralph Hamers by 50 percent, saying that his compensation was well below the median for similar executives. They made the proposal to increase his base salary and also significantly increase his stock remuneration by creating a new classification of fixed stock that was seen to be in compliance with Dutch government regulations. A firestorm of disapproval emerged from customers, employees, and politicians, and ING acted quickly to withdraw the proposal from the annual meeting's agenda in April 2018. The long-term result will be interesting to watch as the company searches for the proper remuneration balance for its executive team (ING 2018d; ING 2018e; Meijer 2018).

Overall, ING's financial success has been sound with stable stock prices and rising profits. Part of this may be due to some innovative governance structures within the company. An article from McKinsey & Company describes an innovative and agile management structure that allows the company to respond to evolving technological offerings and market demand. This seems to fit with ING's goals to plan ahead, look to the future business model, and build structures within the company to promote the best possible solutions (McKinsey & Company 2017).

I invite you to pursue these topics and more as you investigate how good governance, responsible environmental management, and respect for social justice create economic success for ING.

ADDITIONAL RESOURCES

More than one million companies around the world are certified to the ISO 9001 Quality Management standard. It is one of the most popular ISO standards, along with ISO 14001:

- ISO 9001 Quality Management standard: https://www.iso.org/iso-9001 -quality-management.html.

The following document describes the disclosures for reporting against the GRI standard regarding economic performance. This includes management disclosures and topic-specific disclosures regarding direct economic value to stakeholders, financial risks, and opportunities related to climate change, benefit and retirement plans, and governmental assistance:

- GRI 201: Economic Performance 2016: https://www.iso.org/iso-9001 -quality-management.html.

This is a *Harvard Business Review* article. The author argues "don't be evil" is a better guide than "incorporate shared value as a key part of your business strategy:"

- Shared Value versus Don't Be Evil (Weinberger 2011): https://hbr.org/ 2011/04/shared-value-vs-dont-be-evil.

ADDITIONAL CASE RESOURCES

At the following web address you will find links to download the most recent annual report as well as those from previous years. Also found here are previous sustainability reports that were completed before the integrated reporting practice was adopted:

- ING's Annual Reporting landing page: https://www.ing.com/About-us/ Annual-reporting-suite/Annual-Report/2017-Annual-Report-Empow ering-people.htm.

On the ING webpage you will find a wealth of information with various links to more information throughout. It is an easy-to-navigate system with user-friendly guides on how long each page takes to read and options to listen to the text instead of reading it:

- ING's Sustainability webpage: https://www.ing.com/ING-in-society/Sustainability/Our-direction.htm.

This is an interesting article describing the new, more agile structure of management at ING, helping to transform its technologies and stay abreast of new innovations in the banking industry:

- McKinsey & Company. (2017). "ING's agile transformation." McKinsey Quarterly. Retrieved from: https://www.mckinsey.com/industries/financial-services/our-insights/ings-agile-transformation.

QUESTIONS FOR THIS CHAPTER

1. *Environmental management*: What are some of the most effective and innovative areas of environmental impact taken on by ING? How is this driving the market among its competitors? How has partnering with the Ellen MacArthur Foundation opened up opportunities to improve ING's environmental performance? Do its goals seem achievable? How are these goals improving its economic performance? Can you see evidence of shared value in any of the company strategies?
2. *Social responsibility*: Which partners do you think have been the most advantageous for ING regarding social responsibility? What types of investments has ING made in its social value chain and how has that paid off for the company from an economic perspective? How has ING played a leadership role in this area and is it working with competitors or businesses across other industries?
3. *Economic responsibility*: How do the investments in environmental and social responsibility help to improve the bottom line for ING? Has the group had any challenges in making the business case for particular improvements, and, if so, how has it met those challenges? Do you see any evidence of the company's respect for the five capitals in its strategies? How can you see its performance affecting its competitors? Is ING moving the needle for other financial institutions to improve their environmental and social footprints? How about the company's financial investments?

4. *Leadership and strategic planning*: What kinds of internal leadership mechanisms are ING using to promote progress on its goals? How has the recent turmoil over executive compensation affected its approach to leadership and communication about compensation? Take a look at the McKinsey article cited in this chapter and reflect on how ING's new leadership structure can help drive economic performance as well as sustainability for the company.

REFERENCES

Corporate Knights. (2018). "2018 Global 100 Results." Corporate Knights. Retrieved from: http://www.corporateknights.com/magazines/2018-global -100-issue/2018-global-100-results-15166618/.

Fortune. (2018). "Fortune Global 500 List 2018." Retrieved from: http://fortune .com/global500/.

Governance & Accounting Institute, Inc. (G&A Inst.). (2016). "FLASH REPORT: 81% of the S&P 500 Index Companies Published Corporate Sustainability Reports in 2015." Retrieved from: http://www.ga-institute .com/nc/issue-master-system/news-details/article/flash-report-eighty-one -percent-81-of-the-sp-500-index-companies-published-corporate-sustain abi.html.

ING. (2018a). "ING at a glance." Retrieved from: https://www.ing.com/ About-us/Profile/ING-at-a-glance.htm.

ING. (2018b). "Circular economy." Retrieved from: https://www.ing.com/ ING-in-society/Sustainability/Sustainable-business/Circular-economy .htm.

ING. (2018c). "Sustainable business." Retrieved from: https://www.ing.com/ ING-in-society/Sustainability/Sustainable-business.htm.

ING. (2018d). "ING Annual Report 2017: Empowering People." Amsterdam: ING. Retrieved from: https://www.ing.com/ING-in-society/Sustainability/ The-world-around-us-1/Reporting.htm.

ING. (2018e). "ING Supervisory Board withdraws remuneration proposal." Retrieved from: https://www.ing.com/Newsroom/All-news/Press-releases/ ING-Supervisory-Board-withdraws-remuneration-proposal.htm.

Kiron, D., et al. (2013). "Sustainability's next frontier: Walking the talk on the sustainability issues that matter most." *MIT Sloan Management Review* & Boston Consulting Group. Retrieved from: http://sloanreview.mit.edu/ projects/sustainabilitys-next-frontier/.

McKinsey & Company. (2017). "ING's agile transformation." McKinsey Quarterly. Retrieved from: https://www.mckinsey.com/industries/financial-services/our-insights/ings-agile-transformation.

Meijer, B. (2018). "ING's 50 percent pay hike angers Dutch politicians." Reuters. Retrieved from: https://www.reuters.com/article/us-ing-groep-ceo/ing-ceos-50-percent-pay-hike-angers-dutch-politicians-idUSKCN1GK1RI.

Unruh, G., et al. (2016). Investing for a Sustainable Future: Investors Care More about SustainAbility than Many Executives Believe." MIT Sloan Management Review and Boston Consulting Group. Retrieved from: http://sloanreview.mit.edu/projects/investing-for-a-sustainable-future/.

CHAPTER 9

STRATEGY: NESTLÉ AND SHARED VALUE

In this chapter we will investigate the strategy of Nestlé Company and its approach to shared value—a concept introduced by Michael Porter and Richard Kramer in their groundbreaking *Harvard Business Review* article about corporate responsibility in 2006, and later expanded in 2011. In their first article, they cited the example of Nestlé and how they worked with dairy farmers in India to increase value for the company by creating incentives for their suppliers to provide better product and a more secure supply of that product. This was using sustainability strategically. They created a plan and framework that looked at the supply chain from the outside in, and from the inside out. By creating relationships that supported local farmers and also benefited Nestlé, they created a dependable supply of high-quality product.

The work that Nestlé does with dairy farmers in India is a good example of how they have used their value chain to their strategic advantage. In the early 1960s they wanted to expand their business in India and received government permission to operate in Moga, an impoverished area of India. Most farmers owned just one buffalo that provided only enough milk for their own family, and the survival rate of calves was a dismal 50% or less. Nestlé needed a stable supply of milk, so before they could invest in refrigeration and transportation of milk, they needed to help the farmers create a more sustainable supply. They provided training and nutritional supplements for the farmers, helping them improve not only the health of their animals but also the crops they raised to feed the animals.

Over time, production increased and the quality of milk also increased, allowing Nestlé to pay more for the milk produced. This in turn improved the standard of living in Moga and surrounding communities and also provided increased demand for their own products. What started with 180 farmers in the 1960s grew to over 75,000 farmers in 2005. This success has been translated to other areas of the supply chain for Nestlé, including coffee and cocoa production—and including Brazil, Thailand, China, and a dozen other countries around the world (Porter, M. and M. Kramer. 2006).

In their second *Harvard Business Review* article in 2011, Porter and Kramer once again looked at Nestlé, but focused upon their Nespresso division. This time it was coffee that the company wanted to source—premium coffee beans for their production of the Nespresso single cup coffees for their espresso machines. Once again, obtaining a reliable supply of the specialized coffees was a challenge. Most of these coffees are grown in small operations in impoverished areas of Latin America and Africa where production quality is often poor, land degradation common, and procurement difficult.

They invested directly with the farmers to educate them and improve their farming techniques, resulting in better quality and more reliable supply, while also providing a more sustainable agricultural practice to ensure long-term benefit for both the farmer and to Nespresso's supply chain. They provided security for bank loans, advice on fertilizers and plant stock, and they redesigned the procurement methods. This resulted in a more reliable and superior supply of coffee for their product, and by working directly with growers, they were able to pay more for the product—truly a win-win (Porter, M. and M. Kramer. 2011).

Headquartered in Switzerland, Nestlé is the world's largest food and beverage company, comprised of over 2,000 brands, including familiar names such as Nescafé, Gerber, Stouffers, Carnation, Perrier, and Nestea. They also own Friskies and Purina. In 2017, they employed over 323,000 personnel worldwide in 413 factories and in 85 countries, with roughly 90 billion Swiss Francs in sales (about the same in U.S. dollars). They were established over 150 years ago when Henri Nestlé developed an infant food made from cow's milk, flour, and sugar, and later merged with the Anglo-Swiss Condensed Milk Company to form the Nestlé Group. In the first half of the twentieth century, its milk and cocoa products were their staples, but in the last half of the century, they expanded into a wide variety of food products and are now most recently exploring cosmetics and medical nutrition. Their shared value approach is now a centerpiece of their corporate strategy (Nestlé 2018).

Nestlé has a good reputation for its sustainability practices in general, but over the past few years, some local stakeholders have challenged the company for some of its water bottling operations. Some of these criticisms seem short sighted. In California, for example, there were protests outside of Sacramento against Nestlé for their use of groundwater for bottling at what was seen as an unfair low price. Nestlé was operating under a long-time contract that came up for renewal. Critics focused upon Nestlé's use of water, but in comparison to the overall use of water by the city's residents, and the enormous amount of water used in surrounding agriculture, this judgment seemed misaligned (Kaye 2015).

In fact, Nestlé has received high marks from respected organizations such as Ceres for its careful management of water resources and for recognizing the risks of climate change regarding its future availability of water (Ceres 2017).

As you have seen so far, not every company is perfect in its journey toward sustainability. Some do better than others in various areas, but it is rare for a company to be stellar in all three aspects of sustainability and to perform seamlessly with its various stakeholders. Just when things seem to be going swimmingly, another issue pops up on the horizon. Having a resilient management system and strong company culture can help, but that doesn't mean there aren't challenges along the way.

For Nestlé, creating shared value includes a number of strategies, including maximizing economic concerns, but also focusing upon what is most important—using materiality analysis to help decide which areas to focus upon in their value creation. They also emphasize ethical considerations. This can be a real challenge working in countries around the world where cultures may have different value systems, such as traditions for kickbacks and bribes. For a global company, promoting transparency and ethical principles are part of their license to operate, and these issues need constant attention and focus. Nestlé has certainly had its challenges over its history in these areas, and their new emphasis on shared value is helping, but it may take time for the various stakeholder groups to come to an agreement regarding their reputation.

ADDITIONAL RESOURCES

This is the collection of *Harvard Business Review* articles mentioned in Chapter 10 of *Mainstreaming Corporate Sustainability* in the section called Additional Resources:

- *Harvard Business Review: Must Reads on Strategy.* https://www.amazon .com/HBRs-10-Must-Reads-Strategy/dp/1511367075.

The following article was also recommended in Chapter 2, but I'm mentioning it here again in case you missed it:

- *Harvard Business Review:* "Creating Shared Value." Porter and Kramer. (2011). https://hbr.org/2011/01/the-big-idea-creating-shared-value.

This one was mentioned in the previous chapter, but I'm recommending it again here since it relates to the previous article from Porter and Kramer. This is a short piece, but it provides some questions about the challenges of implementing shared value for companies and how the *don't be evil* concept could provide a complementary tool to move businesses toward more responsible behavior:

- Weinberger. "Shared Value vs. Don't Be Evil," (2011): https://hbr.org/2011/04/shared-value-vs-dont-be-evil.

Ceres is a leading nonprofit sustainability organization promoting business responsibility. This roadmap provides a comprehensive strategy for incorporating sustainability throughout an organization. This page also provides a link to the updated version published in 2016:

- Ceres. The 21st Century Corporation, the CERES Roadmap to Sustainability 2010. https://www.ceres.org/resources/reports/21st-century-corporation-ceres-roadmap-sustainability.

Besides this link, you can find various blogs describing the ISO quality management principles and how to implement them:

- ISO 9001: Seven quality management principles: https://www.iso.org/files/live/sites/isoorg/files/archive/pdf/en/pub100080.pdf.

The following is another great article on strategy; it provides some good examples of how a company can determine if a given issue is strategic:

- The Sweet Spot of Sustainability Strategy. *MIT Sloan Management Review*: https://sloanreview.mit.edu/article/the-sweet-spot-of-sustainability-strategy/.

ADDITIONAL CASE RESOURCES

From this page you can download the *Creating Shared Value* report. There are also links to governance, social, and environmental performance and goals:

- Link to Nestlé shared value info: https://www.nestle.com/csv/what-is-csv.

This section provides information focused on Nestlé companies in the United States. It also contains a link to the company's 2015 *Creating Shared Value* report:

- Link to Nestlé USA Shared Value: https://www.nestleusa.com/csv/what-is-csv.

The next article includes an interview with Janet Voûte, global head of public affairs, Nestlé SA, and her comments on Porter and Kramer's concept of shared value. Was it really Nestlé's idea?

- *CR Magazine.* "Creating Shared Value: More old-fashioned than it sounds." https://www.3blassociation.com/insights/creating-shared-value -more-old-fashioned-than-it-sounds.

QUESTIONS FOR THIS CHAPTER

1. *Shared value thread*: How has Nestlé used shared value to further its sustainability strategy? Is this working for more than just the low-hanging fruit, as described in the article by Weinberger in the *Harvard Business Review*? Have you seen other companies using shared value with success?
2. *Strengths and challenges thread*: What are some of the strengths of Nestlé's sustainability program? What are some of its biggest challenges?
3. *Water issues thread*: How has Nestlé responded to the criticisms and protests from local communities regarding its water bottling plants? How have Coca-Cola and other drink manufacturers dealt with these issues?

REFERENCES

Ceres. (2017). "Feeding ourselves thirsty: Tracking food company progress toward a water-smart future." Ceres. Retrieved from: https://www.ceres .org/news-center/press-releases/new-report-ranks-largest-global-food -companies-water-risk-management.

Kaye, L. (2015). "Is the Protest Against Nestlé Bottled Water in California on Point?" Triple Pundit. Retrieved from: https://www.triplepundit.com/ 2015/04/is-the-protest-against-nestle-bottled-water-in-california-on-point/.

Nestlé. (2018). "The Nestlé Company History." Retrieved from: https://www .nestle.com/aboutus/history/nestle-company-history.

Porter, M. and M. Kramer. (2006). "Strategy and society: The link between competitive advantage and corporate social responsibility." *Harvard Business Review, 84*(12): 78–92.

Porter, M. and M. Kramer. (2011). "Creating Shared Value." *Harvard Business Review, 89*(1–2): 62–77.

CHAPTER **10**

SUSTAINABILITY MANAGEMENT AND BMW

BMW—Bayerische Motoren Werke AG, or Bavarian Motor Company Ltd.—was established in 1916 as a company manufacturing aircraft engines. It was briefly called BFW, for Bayerische Flugzeug-Werke, before converting to the more general BMW in 1917. Its classic logo, incorporating the colors of Bavaria and the graphic of an airplane propeller, has endured virtually unchanged since that time. Figure 10.1 shows the subtle changes over the years (BMW, n.d.).

Today, BMW Group boasts three brands: BMW, MINI, and Rolls-Royce. It is headquartered in Munich, Germany and employs roughly 125,000 people worldwide in 31 production and assembly plants in 14 countries, including the United States, the United Kingdom, China, and India. Its revenues in 2016 were €94 billion ($123 billion), up from €92 billion in 2015, and with 2016 net profits of €6.9 billion after taxes (BMW 2016).

Besides its reputation for excellence in quality and innovation, BMW has become widely respected for its commitments to sustainability. It is the only automobile manufacturer to be listed in the Dow Jones Sustainability Index (DJSI) every year since the inception of the DJSI in 1999, and was listed as the leader in its industry in the DJSI from 2005 through 2016. The Carbon Disclosure Project gave BMW an *A* for its measures on climate protection. This makes BMW

Figure 10.1   The BMW logo (BMW, n.d.)

one of only two companies around the world that have been given that rating for seven years consecutively (BMW 2016a).

BMW Group has also benefited from its concentration on the efficient use of resources. Though the company is known for high-performance vehicles, efficiency has more and more become a focus. It has introduced carbon fiber parts into its automobiles, reducing weight, increasing safety, and improving gas mileage. It has publicly declared a goal to halve its 1995 CO_2 emission levels from its vehicles by 2020 (BMW 2016a).

BMW's highly efficient diesel-powered 118d model received the World Green Car of the Year award in 2008. This, along with several other environmental awards, supported BMW's current position at the top of the industry for premium automobiles with excellent environmental performance (Automoto portal.com 2008).

In 2013, BMW introduced its first all-electric vehicle, the BMW i3. With a range of 80 to 100 miles and using its efficient dynamics engineering, the i3 is seen as a pilot project for BMW. The company intends to use the design and manufacture of this model to benchmark its resource use and recycling for its entire product line (BMW 2013). As many sustainability professionals argue, sustainability efforts can help promote resilience in a company. Indeed, BMW maintained its profitability throughout the last recession, unlike many of its competitors (Nica 2013). BMW Group is rated 52nd in the Fortune Global 500 list for 2018 and is in the top 20 of Fortune's *Most Admired* companies of 2018. The selection is made through surveying top executives of industry leaders, and the criteria for rating the companies include many items related to sustainability (Korn Ferry 2018):

1. Ability to attract and retain talented people
2. Quality of management
3. Social responsibility to the community and the environment
4. Innovativeness
5. Quality of products or services
6. Wise use of corporate assets
7. Financial soundness
8. Long-term investment value
9. Effectiveness in doing business globally

BMW has made sustainability a key strategic goal since 2009. In 2003, the company was the subject of two articles published in the *International Journal of Corporate Sustainability*, describing its transition from having a former emphasis on environmental management systems (ISO 14001) to a full sustainability management system (SMS). Links to these papers are provided at the end of this chapter, and you will find them to be interesting reading as you investigate how BMW has continued its journey toward sustainability.

For BMW today, every major project must have measurable sustainability objectives. This means measuring both financial and nonfinancial performance. Managers are compensated according to their achievements toward sustainability performance objectives, making sustainability personal to key members of BMW leadership (BMW 2016a).

BMW's history of environmental responsibility spans decades, including the appointment of its first environmental officer in 1970. In 1999 the company implemented ISO 14001 certification (an environmental certification) throughout its plants. In 2001 it embarked on a company-wide strategy to implement a full SMS. This included key performance indicators of social, environmental, and economic measurements. The SMS was developed around the framework of the ISO 14001 standard, but it included broader targets to include all three aspects of sustainability (Toffel, Hill, and McElhaney 2003).

In this chapter you will have an opportunity to study the journey of BMW on its path toward overall sustainability. It represents the chapter's topic of an SMS well. The company excels in many of the areas that you have studied in this book: a solid business case for sustainability, good governance and ethics, serious engagement of stakeholders across the supply chain, and attention to key performance indicators in environmental, social, and economic aspects. Its sustainability report is easy to navigate and includes links to Global Reporting Initiative reporting information.

It is also interesting to contemplate the progress of BMW in comparison to the scandal that erupted at rival German automaker Volkswagen in 2015 regarding its diesel emissions. BMW has not been implicated in any breach of reporting or tinkering with emission test results. A story briefly surfaced regarding an error in BMW testing, but it appears to have been either a hoax or a mistake. The magazine reporting the test result later retracted the story but not before BMW stock fell almost 10 percent. BMW sells a lot of diesel cars, which makes up 38 percent of the company's total sales (although in the United States, they make up only six percent of autos sold) (Nica 2015).

At the same time, it has come to light since the VW scandal that virtually all diesel automobiles emit more nitrogen oxide (NOx) emissions on the road versus in controlled testing environments. Some BMW automobiles have been found to have NOx emissions greater than allowed under these actual road tests, and four BMW diesel models for 2017 have been delayed due to new stricter Environmental Protection Agency (EPA) testing in the United States. Although these diesel cars emit less CO_2 than regular gasoline engines, NOx is still a powerful greenhouse gas and a health hazard, especially for those people suffering from asthma. Many European cities have strict NOx regulations, and this will be a challenge for diesel car manufacturers going forward (Caparella 2016; Carrington, Topham, and Walker 2016).

This will be an interesting story to watch, and it raises the question of whether a robust SMS at Volkswagen might have prevented the fraudulent testing engineering. How will BMW's sustainability systems management and strategies help this company provide a pathway for its diesel engines? Will it prove more resilient in the face of these challenges?

It is hard to say where the future will take BMW. Its venture into the electric vehicle world is certainly appropriate, but will its customers still demand the roar and feel of a fossil fuel-powered engine? Consumer tastes have certainly changed over the past decade, and Toyota's success with its Prius model is a prime example. Tesla has definitely brought new focus to luxury cars and battery-powered mobility.

Most of us won't have a chance to own a BMW i3 (pictured in Figure 10.2), but you can enjoy getting to know this company that is aiming to be the premium provider of personal mobility. One can only hope that the company might expand its dream to public transportation.

Figure 10.2   BMW i3 electric vehicle (https://www.bmwusa.com)

ADDITIONAL RESOURCES

The following article outlines the importance of strategy and using a management system to keep a company's performance on track. Too many companies that find themselves in trouble focus on short-term solutions and end up missing their goals because they fail to implement strategies, planning, and follow-up of those plans:

- Kaplan and Norton. (2007). "Mastering the Management System." *Harvard Business Review*: https://hbr.org/2008/01/mastering-the-management -system.

This article outlines the institutional logic that distinguishes great companies from those that are merely in business for corporate profit. Kaplan argues that great companies take the long view, invest in their social benefits, and in their leadership provide benefit to mankind as well as to their shareholders:

- Kanter. (2011). "How Great Companies Think Differently." *Harvard Business Review*: https://hbr.org/2011/11/how-great-companies-think -differently.

These are links to previews of these ISO frameworks. ISO 14001 is the Environmental Management standard, ISO 26000 is the Social Responsibility guideline, and ISO 9001 is the Quality Management standard:

- ISO 14001: Environmental responsibility: https://www.iso.org/iso-14001 -environmental-management.html.
- ISO 26000: Social responsibility: https://www.iso.org/iso-26000-social -responsibility.html.
- ISO 9001: Quality management: https://www.iso.org/iso-9001-quality -management.html.

The following scholarly paper compares one thousand companies in California, analyzing the performance between those that implemented ISO 9001 Quality Management and those that did not. They found a significant difference in the corporate survival rate for those that implemented ISO 9001:

- Levine and Toffel. (2010). Management Systems Affect Employees and Employers. https://pubsonline.informs.org/doi/pdf/10.1287/mnsc.1100.1159.

ISO has recently published a guide for implementing ISO 14001 for small and medium-sized companies:

- ISO: A practical guide for SMEs. (2017). https://www.iso.org/publication/ PUB100411.html.

ADDITIONAL CASE RESOURCES

- Toffel, M.W., N. Hill, and K.A. McElhaney. (2005). "Designing a Sustainability Management System at BMW Group." The Designworks/USA Case Study. Greenleaf Publishing. Available at: http://www.people.hbs.edu/mtoffel/publications/mcelhaney_toffel_hill_2006_gmi.pdf.
- BMW website for sustainability: https://www.bmwgroup.com/en/responsibility.html.
- BMW Sustainability Report for 2016: https://www.bmwgroup.com/content/dam/bmw-group-websites/bmwgroup_com/ir/downloads/en/2016/2016-BMW-Group-Sustainable-Value-Report.pdf.
- You can also do an Internet search for the most recent sustainability reports for BMW. They are easily navigated with links to various focus areas.

QUESTIONS FOR THIS CHAPTER

1. *Strategy and planning*: What can you find about the planning stage of the SMS for BMW? How did the company involve the entire corporate system in this planning process? The last chapter focused on strategy; how did BMW's strategy affect its planning process? What challenges did it face and how did it overcome them? What challenges does it continue to wrestle with?
2. *Translating 14001 to an SMS*: What types of problems did BMW find when it tried to translate its ISO 14001 language into the overall SMS for the company? How did it address those problems? How can a company like BMW use its existing management system language to apply to sustainability goals?
3. *Aspects and impacts*: How has BMW translated the ISO aspects and impacts into real language for its management team? What particular aspects and impacts has it focused on and how are these communicated to the various divisions and supply chains? What are the most difficult challenges in the environmental, social, and economic areas?
4. *BMW SMS*: How has the SMS been a driver of success for BMW? What is the most obvious business case for the SMS for BMW? How might having a robust SMS prevent fraudulent activity at BMW, such as was recently found at Volkswagen in its diesel emission engineering? Or how does it compare with other companies we have focused on so far in this book?

REFERENCES

Automotoportal.com. (2008). "BMW 118d Wins World Green Car of the Year." Retrieved from: http://www.automotoportal.com/article/bmw-118d -wins-world-green-car-of-the-year.

BMW. (n.d). "Milestones." BMW Group. Retrieved from: https://www.bmw group.com/en/company/history.html.

BMW. (2013). "Working Together; Sustainable Value Report 2013." BMW Group. Retrieved from: https://www.bmwgroup.com/en.html.

BMW. (2016). "Annual Report 2016." BMW Group. Retrieved from: https:// www.bmw-group.com/content/dam/bmw-group-websites/bmwgroup _com/ir/downloads/en/2016/BMW_GB16_en_Finanzbericht.pdf.

BMW. (2016a). "Sustainable Value Report 2016." BMW Group. https://www .bmwgroup.com/content/dam/bmw-group-websites/bmwgroup_com/ir/ downloads/en/2016/2016-BMW-Group-Sustainable-Value-Report.pdf.

Caparella, J. (2016). "2017 BMW Diesels Delayed Due to Additional EPA Emissions Testing." Car and Driver. Retrieved from: https://www.caranddriver .com/news/2017-bmw-diesels-delayed-due-to-additional-epa-emissions -testing.

Carrington, D., G. Topham, and P. Walker. (2016). "Revealed: nearly all new diesel cars exceed official pollution limits." The Guardian. Retrieved from: goo.gl/fmJSsi.

Korn Ferry. (2018). "Fortune World's Most Admired Companies." Korn Ferry Institute. Retrieved from: https://www.kornferry.com/institute/fortune -worlds-most-admired-companies-2018.

Nica, G. (2013). "BMW Voted Most Admired Car Manufacturer by Fortune Magazine." Autoevolution. Retrieved from: https://www.autoevolution.com/ news/bmw-voted-most-admired-car-manufacturer-by-fortune-magazine -56608.html.

Nica, G. (2015). "BMW Releases Full Statement Regarding Malicious Rumors about Its Diesel Engines." Autoevolution. Retrieved from: https://www .autoevolution.com/news/bmw-releases-full-statement-regarding-malicious -rumors-about-its-diesel-engines-100325.html.

Toffel, M.W., N. Hill, and K.A. McElhaney. (2003). "Developing a Management Systems Approach to Sustainability at BMW Group." (Part 1 of 2 parts). *International Journal of Corporate Sustainability. 10*(2), 2-29–2-39.

CHAPTER 11

SUPPLY CHAIN MANAGEMENT AND ADIDAS GROUP

Now that we have studied the basics of the sustainability management system (SMS) and the tools used to implement an SMS within a company, it is time to expand the SMS to the supply chain, or the value chain, as coined by Michael Porter. It is here that companies can uncover more ways to improve their sustainability footprints: to ensure quality materials and products for their own use, to protect human rights and enforce their codes of conduct with their suppliers, and to develop partnerships in the journey toward sustainability.

In this chapter you will have an opportunity to discover why adidas Group stands out as a leader in supply chain management. The company is deeply engaged with its various stakeholders and has developed strong relationships with nongovernmental organizations (NGOs) in various regions to enhance its ability to improve its supply chain practices. It has employed management systems and codes of conduct to improve its environmental and social performance. The company is committed to transparent reporting on its material issues and has issued a sustainability report for the past 16 years as well as supplementary information on its website. As a result, adidas has thrived as a leading provider of quality athletic shoes and apparel for men and women (adidas Group 2015a).

Headquartered in Germany, adidas Group employs over 60,000 people in over 160 countries to produce their goods. Sales in 2016 totaled €19 billion ($23.4 billion), putting the company at number 468 on the Forbes Global 2000 list for 2017. Its brands include adidas, Reebok, Rockport, and CCN. The adidas Group is strongly respected for its sustainability practices and is rated highly in many sustainability indices, especially as it relates to its supply chain. However, one overall rating company, Corporate Knights, ranked adidas fifth in the world in 2016, but dropped it to number 49 in 2017 and in 2018, adidas didn't even make the list of the top hundred. What happened? In late 2017 and early 2018, a bribery scandal erupted, implicating an adidas employee in the world of NCAA basketball. Although this scandal has not appeared to significantly affect adidas's sales, it may well have impacted its reputation in the sustainability community. This issue is presented in more detail at the end of this chapter. For now, we will focus on the supply chain successes of adidas Group (adidas Group n.d; Forbes 2016; Corporate Knights 2016, 2017, 2018; Root 2018). In 2008 adidas launched its Green Company program, setting targets for energy and water reduction. It met or exceeded those targets as of 2015, including ISO 14001 certification for a number of its sites around the world. In 2015 it developed a new set of targets toward 2020 goals, and in 2016 it implemented an integrated management system to coordinate compliance with three international standards: ISO 14001 (environment), ISO 50001 (energy), and OHSAS 18001 (health and safety). The group is also working toward LEED certification of its stores and offices with the establishment of a venture capital fund to support energy improvements and renewable energy investments worldwide. It is apparently the first of its kind in the apparel and footwear industry (adidas 2015b, 2017).

The adidas Group was one of the original members of the Sustainable Apparel Coalition (SAC), which is working to develop the Higg index. This is a self-assessment tool for the shoe and apparel industry, measuring the environmental and social impact of products, the materials used, the production process, use, and end of life. It uses a spreadsheet of over two hundred inputs to help manufacturers determine the impact of their products. The emphasis is currently on environmental concerns, but it does include some social aspects, and there are plans to incorporate more social metrics as the tool is refined. The adidas Group is still listed as a member of the Higg index, but its current sustainability reporting indicates it is developing a new tool for the footprint of its products and is now piloting that tool as well (adidas Group 2012, 2017; SAC, n.d.).

Compared with other apparel companies, adidas ranks very well regarding its social responsibility in the supply chain, although not as strongly as some, such as Patagonia. As has already been presented in this book, controlling the working conditions in a complicated supply chain can be very difficult. Ensuring that suppliers live up to their commitments to codes of conduct is one part of the challenge, and preventing suppliers from using subcontractors for work is another area that can thwart supply chain controls.

At adidas, a lot of time and effort goes into creating strong relationships with suppliers to ensure that wages and working conditions for laborers meet company expectations. In Indonesia, for example, adidas aligned with other companies to create a Freedom of Association Protocol that supports workers for global brands and gives them the right to associate and bargain for better wages.

This was signed in 2011 and sets a benchmark for the group's suppliers, giving them a clear communication pathway between factory managers and union organizers. This was an important step for adidas, which values the skilled Indonesian labor force that manufactures its Predator football boot.

Another example of responsible supply chain management for adidas is its SMS worker hotline, piloted in 2012 and now covering over 60 percent of its strategic suppliers, including those in Indonesia, Vietnam, China, and Cambodia. It offers a texting service through an independent provider, allowing workers to anonymously express their concerns about factory conditions or harassment.

On the materials side, the group is developing technologies to dye fabric using less water and to grow cotton more sustainably. It found that by setting targets ahead of time with growers and supporting them with training and supply chain support, it was able to greatly improve the sustainability of its cotton supply.

Design is another area where adidas has improved its footprint by reducing waste in the production of its shoes. The Duramo shoe is highlighted in its 2014 sustainability report, showing how computer stitching and revised design decreased the number of pieces in the shoe, reducing waste and improving the product by making it lighter overall (adidas Group 2014).

The 2015 sustainability report for adidas has more stories and vignettes on specific initiatives of the company, but it also has sections that show progress on the company's goals from previous years. This is helpful for the reader who wants to analyze true progress on previous goals rather than just stating new goals each year. For example, in its section on Planet Targets, it analyzes the progress on chemical reduction and carbon footprinting and whether the company has fully achieved or partially achieved its goals (adidas Group 2015a).

It is also important to look at how others are viewing adidas in their sustainability efforts. Given the added scrutiny of apparel industry suppliers after the tragic factory collapse in Bangladesh in 2013, a number of NGOs have participated to improve the conditions and also to monitor the social impacts in the supply chain.

A partnership between the NGOs Baptist World Aid Australia and Not for Sale has rated the apparel industry over the past several years, focusing mostly on the social perspective. Their 2019 report provides a detailed analysis of the top apparel manufacturers, including various stages of manufacturing from raw materials to cut and trim, including both environmental and social impacts. This report provides a good perspective on the complexity of the subject as well as the opportunities for improvement.

The adidas Group was given an overall A rating in this report, up from a B+ a few years ago. It has performed well compared to many of its peers in the footwear industry, including Nike (rated B– in the 2019 report, up from a C+ in 2017). The report recognized adidas for its traceability and transparency, particularly in the cut-and-trim portion of the supply chain. The company still has work to do in other areas, such as cotton production and other textile inputs.

Although adidas rates highly in the areas of policies (codes of conduct, responsible purchasing, and subcontracting policies), transparency, and environmental management, it has challenges in the area of worker empowerment (Baptist World Aid Australia 2019). Figure 11.1 shows how adidas compares to some of the other major apparel companies as analyzed in the Baptist World Aid Australia report from 2019.

A link to the reports from Baptist World Aid is provided at the end of this chapter. There you can more clearly see additional tables and figures comparing the companies and highlighting some of the challenges facing supply chain management regarding workers' rights and labor relations.

As we saw in the first half of this book, environmental effects can have social impacts as well. Energy use impacts climate change, growing cotton can have devastating effects on the land and the workers in the field, and the processing and dying of fabrics are water intensive and can cause terrible pollution that impacts drinking water for downstream populations. The adidas Group has taken on these issues and understands its supply chain responsibilities in this area. It has partnered with the SAC in the production of the Higg index, as previously mentioned. For chemicals, it works with bluesign® technologies to screen and manage the use of chemicals in its supply chain. It has a goal to phase out the use of perfluorinated compounds (PFCs) that are commonly used in athletic attire to repel water and dirt. Finally, its Green Company Program supports a universal EMS program across the company, utilizing various international standards (adidas Group 2014, 2017).

NCAA BRIBERY SCANDAL

In the fall of 2017, adidas Group was implicated in a bribery scandal involving high school athletes. Jim Gatto, director of global sports and marketing for adidas Group, was arrested for allegedly funneling hundreds of thousands of dollars to high school athletes to encourage them to enroll in colleges that had contracts with adidas. Gatto has been placed on administrative leave, and adidas has been relatively quiet about its response to the charges. Nine others were also charged, including an independent contractor working for Gatto and four assistant coaches at major universities around the country. Information about this case was still evolving as this book went to press, but the interesting part is

	Policies	Traceability & Transparency	Monitoring & Training	Worker Rights Grade	Overall Grade
VF Corporation	B+	B	A-	D	B
Timberland	B+	A-	A-	C	B+
Skechers USA*	B-	F	F	F	D-
Puma	B+	A-	B+	D	B
Patagonia	A+	A-	A-	B-	A-
Nike	A-	B+	B+	C-	B
New Balance	B	B	B	C+	B-
Lululemon Athletica	B+	A-	A-	C+	B+
Levi Strauss & Co	A	B+	A-	D+	B+
Lacoste	B+	B	B+	D-	B
Kmart	A-	B-	B	D-	B
H&M	A+	A-	A-	B	A-
Gap Inc.	A-	B	B+	D+	B
Fruit of the Loom	A+	A	A	B+	A
Forever New	B-	B-	C+	D-	C+
Apparel Group	D+	D-	D	F	D-
Adidas	A	A-	A-	C	B+
Abercrombie & Fitch*	C+	C-	B-	D-	C

*Non-responsive companies

Figure 11.1 Overall apparel ratings (detail) (Baptist World Aid Australia 2019)

that the scandal does not seem to be impacting adidas's sales overall. Its share of the basketball sales market is relatively small compared to Nike and Under Armour, and the consumer awareness of this issue seems to be low.

The athletic shoe market is extremely competitive, and it is a high-stakes game, with top professional athletes securing multimillion-dollar contracts for sponsorship. Michael Jordan apparently wanted to sign with adidas early in his career, but adidas passed on the deal, and he instead went to Nike, where he, of course, brought great success. Nike has also reportedly signed a lifetime deal with LeBron James that approaches $1 billion. But adidas has managed to sign other players from other sports and has also branched out into the entertainment industry, involving Kanye West and Kendall Jenner (Bieler 2015; Manning 2017; Root 2018).

This will be an area to watch. How will the ethics of sponsorships and bribery charges affect the overall reputation of adidas and other sportswear companies? I invite you to investigate these issues and more as your questions for this chapter.

ADDITIONAL RESOURCES

There are various supply chain guides available, but the one posted here is well written with clear graphics and comes from solid partners in the field:

- "Supply Chain Sustainability: A Practical Guide for Continuous Improvement." (2010). UNGC and BSR. Available at: https://www.bsr.org/reports/BSR_UNGC_SupplyChainReport.pdf.

The following report builds on the preceding guide by providing what is happening on the ground now. Through surveys with 70 global companies, EY (formerly Ernst & Young) worked with the United Nations Global Compact (UNGC) to find an increasingly shared commitment and transparency with its suppliers. Progress beyond the Tier 1 suppliers remains a challenge, but the innovative use of technology is helping to resolve some of these issues:

- "The State of Sustainable Supply Chains." (2016). UNGC and EY. Available at: http://www.unglobalcompact.org/docs/issues_doc/supply_chain/state-of-sustainable-supply-chains.pdf.

You can see from the two previous reports that the UNGC is concentrating on this area. Its website has a number of links to additional resources and case studies. It is a wealth of information for you to utilize on this subject and in your continued studies:

- UNGC supply chain website: https://www.unglobalcompact.org/what-is-gc/our-work/supply-chain.

This article was recommended in the chapter on strategy, but you may have missed it. It is also highly relevant to the supply chain:

- Porter and Kramer. (2011). "Creating Shared Value." Available at: https://hbr.org/2011/01/the-big-idea-creating-shared-value.

The following questionnaire shows the types of questions that would be appropriate for a company to use in evaluating its suppliers. As the document states, it is not a means to an end, but rather a tool to help strengthen relationships with current and future suppliers:

- Ceres supplier self-assessment questionnaire (SAQ). (2012). Available from: https://www.ceres.org/sites/default/files/tool/2017-03/ceres_SAQ.pdf.

ADDITIONAL CASE RESOURCES

The adidas Group has produced sustainability reports since 1998. Since 2012 it has selected indicators that align with the Global Reporting Initiative (GRI) indicators despite the fact that it does not include all this in its sustainability reports. The company has its own reasoning for what should be included in the sustainability report. Beginning in 2017, it initiated a one-report practice, including its sustainability reporting in its annual report and supplementing this with more information on its website. You'll find its reporting to be clearly organized and noting progress on various goals:

- Link to "2017 Annual Report." https://report.adidas-group.com/#1.
- "Sustainability Reporting Section of Annual Report." https://report.adidas-group.com/media/pdf/EN/adidas_AR_2017_Sustainability_EN.pdf.

The adidas website is rich with links to various areas including the supply chain. More and more companies are using a combination of annual reports and online information that can provide more detail and updated reporting:

- https://www.adidas-group.com/en/sustainability/managing-sustainability/general-approach/.

Baptist World Aid Australia surveys the supply chain of the world's leading apparel companies, showing various comparisons of apparel companies. Each year they pull out case studies on various companies. You'll also find many more tables and figures showing the hot spots of labor issues around the world:

- https://baptistworldaid.org.au/.

Another organization, Know the Chain, publishes its own report on apparel and footwear. They also publish reports on information and communications technology as well as food and beverage companies. You may find this an additional helpful resource:

- https://knowthechain.org/.

For more information regarding the NCAA bribery scandal, you can begin with these three articles, including one regarding Nike. There may be additional information available at the time you read this book.

- Manning, J. (2017). "When it came to selling basketball shoes, Gatto, Adidas, shot airball." The Oregonian. Retrieved from: http://www .oregonlive.com/business/index.ssf/2017/10/post_258.html.
- Neumeister, L. (2019). "3 convicted in college bribery scandal get prison sentences," PBS News Hour. Retrieved from: https://www.pbs.org/ newshour/nation/3-convicted-in-college-basketball-bribery-scandal -get-prison-sentences.
- Tracey, M. and K. Draper. (2019). "A Star's Shoe Breaks, Putting College Basketball Under a Microscope." The New York Times. Retrieved from: https://www.nytimes.com/2019/02/21/sports/zion-nike-shoe-ncaa.html.

QUESTIONS FOR THIS CHAPTER

1. *Energy and climate*: What types of innovative measures has adidas taken to reduce its CO_2 emissions in its supply chain? What kind of progress is it making in its efforts to conserve energy and reduce CO_2 emissions? Is the company using normalized metrics or absolute metrics? How does adidas compare with some of the other companies we have studied thus far?

2. *Natural resources and efficiency*: How has adidas traced its materials throughout its supply chain? How does this compare with Levi Strauss or Patagonia? Are there particular areas where adidas has excelled in reducing its impact on the world's resources? What areas of the life cycle are the most challenging, and how is adidas addressing those challenges? How has it made a business case for these improvements?

3. *Workforce and communities*: What are some of the company's strengths regarding its social responsibility in the supply chain? How has it accomplished these successes? What are some of the remaining challenges for the group and can you find evidence of its efforts to address these challenges? What is it doing in the communities where its factories are located? How is it working with NGOs or other local stakeholders? What is the business case for these actions?
4. *Tools and methods*: How is adidas using ISO 14001 to improve its supply chain impacts? Are there other standards or frameworks that it is utilizing to improve performance across the supply chain? Which partnerships have been particularly valuable?
5. *Bribery scandal*: How has adidas responded to the recent scandal in its basketball shoe department? Has it been transparent in its reporting of this issue? Has it affected the company's credibility in the sustainability field?

REFERENCES

adidas Group. (n.d.). "Profile." Retrieved April 15, 2018, from: http://www.adidas-group.com/en/group/profile/.

adidas Group. (2012). "Sustainable apparel coalition launches Higg index." Retrieved from: https://www.adidas-group.com/en/media/news-archive/press-releases/2012/sustainable-apparel-coalition-launches-higg-index/.

adidas Group. (2014). "2014 Sustainability Progress Report: Performance Counts." adidas Group. Retrieved from: https://www.adidas-group.com/media/filer_public/e8/32/e832823b-8585-4e26-8990-07b80e3ae71c/2014_sustainability_report_make_a_difference.pdf.

adidas Group. (2015a). "2015 Sustainability Progress Report: How We Create Responsibly." adidas Group. Retrieved from: https://www.adidas-group.com/en/sustainability/reporting/sustainability-reports/#/2015/.

adidas Group. (2015b). "Green Company Performance Analysis 2015." adidas Group. Retrieved from: http://www.adidas-group.com/media/filer_public/cf/b9/cfb97352-a974-403c-b111-2dfa1dc94d05/green_company_performance_analysis_2015.pdf.

adidas Group. (2017). "adidas Annual Report 2017: Sustainability." adidas Group. Retrieved from: https://report.adidas-group.com/media/pdf/EN/adidas_AR_2017_Sustainability_EN.pdf.

Baptist World Aid Australia. (2019). The 2019 Ethical Fashion Report: The Truth Behind the Barcode. Retrieved from: https://baptistworldaid.org.au/resources/2019-ethical-fashion-report/.

Bieler, D. (2015). "A young Michael Jordan wanted Adidas for his shoe deal. Adidas passed." The Washington Post. Retrieved from: https://www .washingtonpost.com/news/early-lead/wp/2015/03/24/a-young-michael -jordan-wanted-adidas-for-his-shoe-deal-adidas-passed/?noredirect=on &utm_term=.4719cbd5f43b.

Corporate Knights. (2016). "2016 Global 100 Results." Retrieved from: http://www.corporateknights.com/reports/global-100/2016-global-100 -results-14533333/.

Corporate Knights. (2017). "2017 Global 100 Results." Retrieved from: http://www.corporateknights.com/magazines/2017-global-100-issue/ 2017-global-100-results-14846083/.

Corporate Knights. (2018). "2018 Global 100 Results." Retrieved from: https://www.corporateknights.com/magazines/2018-global-100-issue/ 2018-global-100-results-15166618/.

Forbes. (2016). The world's biggest public companies. Forbes. Retrieved April 15, 2018, from: http://www.forbes.com/global2000/list/.

Manning, J. (2017). "When it came to selling basketball shoes, Gatto, Adidas, shot airball." The Oregonian. Retrieved from: https://www.oregonlive .com/business/2017/10/post_258.html.

Nimbalker, G., et al. (2015). "Apparel Industry Trends 2015: The Truth Behind the Barcode." Baptist World Aid Australia in partnership with Not for Sale. Retrieved from: http://www.humanthreadcampaign.org/wp-content/uploads/ 2016/07/Free2Work-Apparel-Industry-Trends-2015.pdf.

Nimbalker, G., et al. (2017). "Apparel Industry Trends 2017: The Truth Behind the Barcode." Baptist World Aid Australia in partnership with Not for Sale. Retrieved from: https://sustainable-textile-school.com/wp-content/ uploads/2017/04/2017-Ethical-Fashion-Report.pdf.

Root, T. (2018). Adidas has gotten a boost. The Washington Post. Retrieved from: https://www.myajc.com/sports/adidas-has-gotten-boost/6s7M0Ladq mudJkAsVeBzAM/.

Sustainable Apparel Coalition (SAC). (n.d.). "Higg Index." Retrieved Oct. 30, 2016, from: http://apparelcoalition.org/the-higg-index/.

CHAPTER 12

SUSTAINABILITY METRICS: CONSIDERING MATERIALITY AT MARKS & SPENCER

INTRODUCTION: MATERIALITY

With this chapter's topic of sustainability metrics, we would like you to think about how companies choose what to report regarding their sustainability results and how they actually communicate those results.

We have already discussed some important topics, including resource efficiency and emissions, workforce relations and productivity, stakeholder engagement, and supply chain management. But how can companies track this information as well as report on it to the company's stakeholders in a coherent manner? What are their stakeholders most interested in hearing about, and how can it be presented in a way that makes sense and also satisfies essential goals of transparency?

The Global Reporting Initiative (GRI) has developed Sustainable Reporting Standards that have been widely recognized as valuable sustainability tools. The standards, released by GRI in October 2016, were originally developed as guidelines and replaced the GRI G4 Guidelines as of July 10, 2018. The standards have an increased emphasis on materiality. The result of this emphasis is that rather than reporting on all or part of the various aspects listed in the original GRI guidelines, the organization uses an analysis called *materiality* to determine the threshold for whether a certain aspect should be reported.

Materiality involves looking at the various areas of impact for a company and analyzing which are most important to report on. The GRI standards outline materiality analysis and the basic principles of reporting to ensure appropriate scope, comprehensibility, and comparability across various sustainability reports. There is a link to the latest GRI standards at the end of this chapter.

The principles of the GRI include the following (GRI 2016) content:

- *Stakeholder inclusiveness*: identify stakeholders and describe how the report responds to their interests
- *Sustainability context*: report regarding the specific context of the organization
- *Materiality*: include significant environmental, social, and economic impacts or significant stakeholder concerns
- *Completeness*: this includes time, scope, and boundaries identified according to stakeholder concerns

QUALITY

- *Accuracy*: metrics should enable stakeholders to verify the information and performance
- *Balance*: include positive and negative assessments to provide an objective overview
- *Clarity*: information should be accessible to a wide variety of stakeholders
- *Comparability*: metrics should be used to enable reasonable assessment over time and to compare results accordingly
- *Reliability*: stakeholders should have assurance that the information presented is correct
- *Timeliness*: there should be a regular schedule of reporting to enable stakeholders to make informed decisions

In the section on materiality, the GRI standards emphasize that reporting on information may include items that are not necessarily strong concerns of the organization itself, but may instead be concerns of outside stakeholders. This may make an item material for reporting purposes. Figure 12.1 shows how material aspects should be determined according to the GRI—the items in the upper right-hand areas of the graph are those most material for reporting (GRI 2016).

The reading materials referenced at the end of this chapter describe various techniques to determine materiality for a company's reporting. There is a multistep process listed in the GRI standards, but sometimes it helps to have another perspective to understand how a process works. AccountAbility suggests the following process for determining the material aspects for a company to report (Murninghan, M., and T. Grant. 2013).

1. Develop a long list of possible issues and then include multiple stakeholders to analyze those issues—both inside and outside the organization.

2. Prioritize the issues, based once again on both internal and external factors, and scale various issues based on the importance (benefit and/ or risk) of various stakeholder interests.
3. Review the analysis through a third-party advisory group and approve the list at the board level.
4. Embed the materiality process into the company's management systems through strategy, stakeholder engagement, performance frameworks, and reporting.

What is material for one company may be very different for another. Subsidiaries and divisions of companies are even beginning to prepare their own sustainability reports so that they can better include information that is more appropriate for their operations and locales.

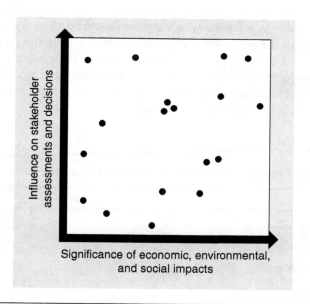

Figure 12.1   GRI prioritization of aspects (GRI 2016)

Determining what is material is often a group exercise including company employees and various stakeholders. Various topics can be charted on a sliding scale according to their importance to stakeholders and their impact on the company, and the top tier of topics can be prioritized accordingly.

Although material issues can vary, there are also some common factors, such as good governance, climate change, use of resources, and attention to human rights. Ceres is a leading nongovernmental organization that is mentioned several times in this book. Ceres was behind the initial adoption of the GRI and has published a report, "The 21st Century Corporation: The Ceres Roadmap to Sustainability," that I'm providing as suggested reading in this chapter (once again) because of its relevance.

The Ceres report contains some suggested indicators for most companies, including specific goals for greenhouse gas emissions and reporting through the GRI. This list could serve as a starting point for any company in its effort to determine the most material issues. A link to the 20 Ceres key expectations is referenced in the additional resources section for this case.

The earlier GRI G4 Guidelines provided a view of how the materiality selection process proceeds, shown in Figure 12.2.

In this process, Step 1 includes applying the principles of inclusiveness and context to determine the various aspects for reporting. Step 2 utilizes the principle of materiality to prioritize which aspects should be reported. Step 3 applies the principles of completeness and inclusiveness to ensure the correct aspects have been selected for reporting. After the report is released, Step 4 instructs the organization to review the report with stakeholders to determine how the next reporting cycle can be improved and whether important material aspects should be updated or revised (GRI 2013a).

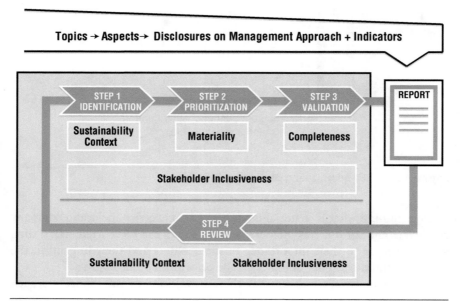

Figure 12.2 Defining material aspects and boundaries—process overview (GRI 2013a)

MARKS & SPENCER

Finally, we're getting to the case! Figure 12.3 shows a materiality analysis chart from Marks & Spencer (M&S)—our case company for this chapter. In its sustainability report, Plan A, from 2016 (M&S 2016a) and in subsequent updates, the company describes a similar process as previously outlined to develop the material issues for its report. M&S started by identifying important issues with stakeholders and then prioritized the issues with management according to the relative importance to stakeholders and to the company itself. Working with DNV GL, it developed a list of about 40 issues that were of highest importance to both outside stakeholders and the company and then had the results from those issues independently assured through either AA1000 AS or IASE 3000 standards. All of the remaining issues were audited internally.

M&S is based in the United Kingdom with sales in 2017 topping £10.6 billion (or $12.4 billion). It is ranked number 1,845 in the 2017 Forbes Global 2000 and is regularly ranked at the top of various lists for its sustainability practices, including ranking number 21 in the Corporate Knights Global 100 for 2016. The company was not listed in 2018 for Corporate Knights but was ranked at 32 in the Forbes sustainability list for 2018. As you can see, these ratings move around (M&S 2018a; Forbes 2017; Forbes 2018; Corporate Knights 2016).

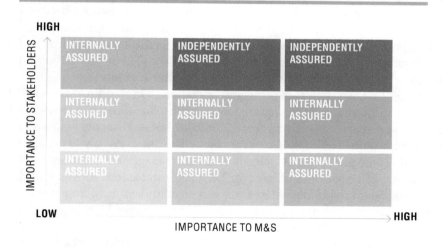

Figure 12.3   M & S materiality reporting (M&S 2016a)

M&S, founded in 1884 as a single stall in London—in what nowadays would be called a mall—today employs roughly 83,000 people worldwide and provides food and general merchandise from 2,200 global suppliers (M&S 2016a). The company is known for its high-quality products and provides easy access to its sustainability goals on its website.

Sustainability has been increasingly important at M&S over the past few decades, and it has received a number of awards and accolades for its progress in this area. But until about 10 years ago, it was mostly cherry-picking in various areas, reducing obvious risks here and taking advantage of efficiencies there. In 2006, then CEO Stuart Rose directed the sustainability team to get serious about its efforts and make them a driving force for the company, embedding sustainability throughout M&S and its supply chain. This brought about the first Plan A, which set at first 100 and then 180 targets across the company to improve its impacts on climate, water, energy, resources, and human well-being by 2015, and embedded sustainability into every area of the company. The effect was to essentially inspire products across the company that supported these goals, such as organic cotton clothing and sustainably caught fish products that its consumers wanted anyway and that the company had the capability to provide (Nichols 2013a).

Plan A for 2014 honed the targets back down to one hundred, a more manageable number to report on and also most likely due to the GRI emphasis on materiality (the 2014 report was the first to follow the GRI G4 Guidelines). In 2015 the report format was revised to follow the basic categories of economic, social, environmental, and supply chain for the GRI framework. In its recent reports, M&S emphasizes its business case for sustainability, disclosing £160 million net income from its sustainability efforts for 2014 and £185 million (or $230 million) in 2015. It is the first retailer to be certified by the Carbon Trust for three standards—water, energy, and waste—and it claims to be the world's only major retailer with carbon-neutral operations. On the climate side, M&S tracks both normalized (per square foot) and absolute CO_2 emissions—down 39 and 31 percent, respectively, from 2006/2007 levels. Diversity is also a hallmark, with women holding 36 percent of board positions (versus 19 percent for S&P 500 companies) and 41 percent of senior management positions (versus 25 percent of senior-level officers for S&P 500 companies). As you will find when you take a closer look, M&S takes sustainability seriously, from inside the company to outside, bringing style and flavor to the sustainability picture (M&S 2014; M&S 2015; M&S 2016a; Catalyst 2016).

Part of the goal for Plan A 2014 for M&S was to further embed the program within the company rather than having it be an add-on silo or separate bureaucracy. Mike Barry, head of sustainable business at M&S, saw it this way:

"The first 180 commitments [were] about making individual parts of the business less bad—less energy, less waste, less packaging, better standards of cotton, wood, etc. But they've all been individual silos. The next step is to start to look at M&S as an ecosystem and how you go from a less bad business to a better business" (Nichols 2013b).

In 2016, M&S achieved its goal of integrated reporting, showing the connection between the environmental and social responsibilities and its financial results. It has done this according to the International Integrated Reporting Council's Integrated Reporting Framework. M&S reported according to the GRI G4 Guidelines, but throughout the 2016 Plan A report, you will see references to its annual report (M&S 2016a). In the next chapter's case, you will see another example of integrated reporting with Novo Nordisk, which has combined its sustainability and annual reports into one overall report.

Besides the integrated report from 2016, M&S published a separate human rights report. This is the first such report for M&S, and the company seems to be forthright about working to resolve some of the tough challenges in its supply chain. The emphasis in the report is on individual rights more than general business risk, and it breaks the major components down to include the following: discrimination, forced labor, freedom of association, health and safety, living wages, water and sanitation, and working hours (M&S 2016b).

M&S has achieved many of its human rights goals in its first-tier supply chain, but the lower tiers remain a challenge—and this is true of many companies, as you have already seen so far. Part of the problem is that local laws in some of these places conflict with the basic human rights principles for the company—and indeed for the rest of the developed world. This will be a very interesting area to watch to see if M&S provides real leadership in this challenging area and if it can engage the suppliers who have previously resisted compliance in the company's quest for a responsible supply chain.

It can also be helpful to review the past years of sustainability reporting for M&S. You can see that in 2013 it was quite extensive, with many goals and results organized under seven pillars. In 2014 the company tried to be more concise by reorganizing the goals under four headings: Inspiration, Intouch, Integrity, and Innovation. In 2015 it reorganized the goals once again under the more traditional categories of Economic, Environmental, Social, and Supply Chain, saying it was in response to reader comments. In 2016 M&S stuck with the same categories, but the four I's (Inspiration, etc.) appear here and there as a theme for the company. As you can see, striking the right balance between splash and professionalism can be a challenge, even for a well-heeled company such as M&S.

We encourage you to delve into the materiality and metrics of M&S as described in this chapter and see how the more recent reports have refined and expanded its disclosures. How does M&S compare with other companies you have studied so far in this book?

ADDITIONAL RESOURCES

GRI Sustainability Reporting Standards—Released in October 2016

As of July 1, 2018, the GRI requires reporting to be performed under GRI Sustainability Reporting Standards rather than the G4 Guidelines. You will find an overview and introduction to the standards, as well as links to download the materials, at this address:

- https://www.globalreporting.org/standards/.

Materiality Report II—AccountAbility 2013

Redefining Materiality II: Why It Matters, Who's Involved, and What It Means for Corporate Leaders and Boards—this report from AccountAbility outlines the various reasons that materiality has risen to the top of corporate sustainability reporting. It provides tools for corporate leaders to make sense of hundreds of data points, along with requests for performance from analysts. You can download the report at this link:

- www.accountability.org/our-services/research/.

The 21st Century Corporation: The Ceres Roadmap for Sustainability (2016)

The Ceres Roadmap published in 2010 contains 20 key expectations. Among other things, these expectations help a company determine material issues for reporting. They are listed in Appendix 6.1 and you can also find them at this link:

- https://www.ceres.org/sites/default/files/2018-02/ceres-rfs-8.5x11-rd7 -v1-1-sm_updated.pdf.

Ceres is the organization responsible for the launching of the Global Reporting Initiative. The Ceres Roadmap is a good document for your long-term reference. You can find updates on this document and more information at the Ceres website:

- https://www.ceres.org/roadmap.

ADDITIONAL CASE RESOURCES

M&S Plan A began in 2007 and there have been annual reports on its progress since then:

- M&S Plan A reports: http://planareport.marksandspencer.com/.

The 2016 M&S Human Rights Report was the first of its kind for M&S, and the company has promised to update it annually through its website and the Plan A reporting. An update was published in 2017. It provides more detail on the analysis of its supply chain from the perspective of workers' rights:

- M&S Human Rights Report 2016. Available at: https://corporate.marks andspencer.com/documents/plan-a-our-approach/mns-human-rights -report-june2016.pdf.
- M&S Human Rights Report 2017. Available at: https://corporate.marks andspencer.com/documents/plan-a-our-approach/mns-human-rights -report-june2017.pdf.

The following webpage provides an online version of the current M&S Annual Report as well as links to downloads of the annual reports and a number of other focused reports:

- M&S annual reporting webpage: http://annualreport.marksandspencer .com/.

QUESTIONS FOR THIS CHAPTER

1. *Materiality*: What are some of the most important material issues to M&S as they relate to its stakeholders? How is the company communi-cating about these issues and how is it tracking their progress? Where the company has not made progress, what kinds of explanations is it providing? How does this compare with other companies we have con-sidered so far in this book?
2. *Metrics*: What types of metrics is M&S using to track important as-pects? Are they clearly identified and explained? Can you find metrics that are qualitative rather than quantitative for certain types of results? If so, how is M&S explaining these metrics? What are the key metrics for its environmental reporting? What about its social reporting?
3. *Business case*: Besides the overall net savings number, what evidence can you find to support the M&S business case for sustainability? How does the company relate its sustainability metrics to financial gain?

How does it use its metrics to speak to consumers regarding the value of the M&S sustainability programs?

4. *Ceres key expectations*: Compare the Ceres key expectations in Appendix 6.1 to the items reported by M&S. Are there any that are missing? If so, can you find a reasonable explanation? Or are they combined with other items that are reported?

REFERENCES

Catalyst. (2016). "Pyramid: Women in S&P 500 Companies." New York, NY: Catalyst. Retrieved from: http://www.catalyst.org/knowledge/women-sp-500-companies.

Ceres. (2016). "The Ceres Roadmap for Sustainability." Retrieved from: https://www.ceres.org/resources/reports/the-ceres-roadmap-for-sustainability-revised-expectations/view.

Corporate Knights. (2016). "2016 Global 100 Results." Retrieved from: http://www.corporateknights.com/magazines/2016-global-100-issue/2016-global-100-results-14533333/.

European Federation of Financial Analysts Societies (EFFAS). (2009). "KPIs for ESG: Key Performance Indicators for Environmental, Social and Governance Issues, Version 1.2." Frankfurt, Germany: EFFAS.

Forbes. (2017). "The World's Most Sustainable Companies." Forbes. Retrieved from: https://www.forbes.com/sites/jeffkauflin/2017/01/17/the-worlds-most-sustainable-companies-2017/#44db40224e9d.

Forbes. (2018). "The World's Largest Public Companies." Forbes. Retrieved from: http://www.forbes.com/global2000/list/.

Global Reporting Initiative (GRI). (2013a). G4 Sustainability Recording Guidelines: Reporting Principles and Standard Disclosures. Amsterdam, Netherlands: Global Reporting Initiative.

Global Reporting Initiative (GRI). (2016). "GRI 101: Foundation 2016. Amsterdam, Netherlands: Global Reporting Initiative." Retrieved from: https://www.globalreporting.org/standards/media/1036/gri-101-foundation-2016.pdf.

Marks & Spencer (M&S). (2014). "Your M&S: Plan A Report 2014." M&S. Retrieved from: http://planareport.marksandspencer.com.

Marks & Spencer (M&S). (2015). "Plan A Report 2015." M&S. Retrieved from: http://planareport.marksandspencer.com/M&S_PlanAReport2015.pdf.

Marks & Spencer (M&S). (2016a). "Plan A Report 2016." M&S. Retrieved from: http://corporate.marksandspencer.com/plan-a-our-approach/89db73e54804477bb1e2b52e09306e43.

Marks & Spencer (M&S). (2016b). "Human Rights Report." M&S. Retrieved from: https://corporate.marksandspencer.com/documents/plan-a-our-approach/mns-human-rights-report-june2016.pdf.

Marks & Spencer (M&S). (2018a). "Annual Report." Retrieved from: https://corporate.marksandspencer.com/annualreport.

Marks & Spencer (M&S). (2018b). "Listening and Taking Action: Delivering Plan A." Retrieved from: https://corporate.marksandspencer.com/plan-a/delivering-plan-a/listening-and-taking-action#7d386df9b35044a58f014d8f89b4b4ca.

Moffat, A. and A. Newton. (2010). "The 21st Century Corporation: The Ceres Roadmap to Sustainability." Ceres. Retrieved from: http://www.ceres.org/resources/reports/ceres-roadmap-to-sustainability-2010.

Murninghan, M. and T. Grant. (2013). Redefining materiality II: Why it matters, who's involved, and what it means for corporate leaders and boards. AccountAbility. Retrieved from: https://www.accountability.org/wp-content/uploads/2017/02/Redefining-Materiality-2.pdf.

Nichols, W. (2013a). "How M&S is making sustainability pay—part one." BusinessGreen. Retrieved from: http://www.businessgreen.com/bg/feature/2286363/how-m-s-is-making-sustainability-pay-part-one.

Nichols, W. (2013b). "How M&S is making sustainability pay—part two." BusinessGreen. Retrieved from: http://www.businessgreen.com/print_article/bg/feature/2286369/how-m-s-is-making-sustainability-pay-part-two.

CHAPTER 13

REPORTING ON SUSTAINABILITY:
NOVO NORDISK

Novo Nordisk is headquartered in Denmark and is a leading global healthcare company, primarily providing insulin for diabetes patients. The company also manufactures products for hemophilia, growth hormone therapy, and hormone replacement therapy. With a 90-year history, the company attests to a commitment to the triple bottom line and is widely recognized for its superior sustainability performance.

In addition to reporting on overall profits and return in its annual report, Novo Nordisk also focuses on the number of people served who have diabetes (26.8 million) and the millions of tons of CO_2 avoided. In 2014 it reported 45 percent in absolute CO_2 reductions since 2004, despite growth of over 200 percent. In 2015 its energy use went up, but its CO_2 emissions still went down, and the company set a new goal to be 100 percent renewable in its operations by 2020. Novo Nordisk was rated number 376 on the Forbes Global 2000, with annual revenues of $17 billion in 2017. They were rated number 19 out of the top 100 global companies on the Corporate Knights list for 2016, but did not appear on the lists for 2017 or 2018 (Novo Nordisk 2014; Novo Nordisk 2015a; Forbes 2018; Corporate Knights 2016). Part of the reasoning for focusing upon Novo Nordisk as our case company in this chapter is because the company has used integrated financial and sustainability reporting over the past decade, and beginning in 2014, it decided to rely primarily on this system for its Corporate Social Responsibility (CSR) reporting rather than publishing a separate Global Reporting Initiative (GRI)-based report. "Oh, no," you may say, "I just got used to the GRI format!" Well, welcome to the sustainability field, a never-ending dodge and play of how to set appropriate goals and report on them.

Integrated reporting is more than just adding social and environmental aspects to the annual financial results. It involves showing and explaining the interconnections between the financial, social, and environmental results. Providing a more holistic view of corporate results helps stakeholders to better understand long-term goals and results and perhaps also short-term costs as well as investments in society and the earth's ecosystems (Biesener 2011).

Novo Nordisk uses materiality analysis to determine the most important information to share in its annual report, linking environmental and social concerns with economic results. It has also published a separate report on its progress with the United Nations Global Compact (UNGC) goals, which it says includes many of the GRI indicators. However, the report is not organized according to those indicators per se. If you are interested, you can find the most recent GRI-based report from Novo Nordisk on the Internet which it reported under the previous GRI 3 framework, with an A rating because of the company's full reporting (Novo Nordisk 2015b; Novo Nordisk 2012).

In its annual report from 2015, you can see from the outset that Novo Nordisk is linking social, environmental, and financial results. In Figure 13.1, found on page five of the report, the company highlights the number of people served by its product as well as the CO_2 emission reductions. Over the past couple of years, Novo Nordisk has come close to its CO_2 and water targets, though not always achieving them. That the company is up front and transparent about these goals and metrics is, of course, important to its stakeholders.

Figure 13.1 illustrates one of the important links that Novo Nordisk is trying to show in its reporting. In 2011, it decided to show the number of patients it serves rather than just the amount of diabetes drug it has sold or the number of people suffering from the disease. This relates to its goal of healing people rather than just selling more products. Since this number was first reported, the company began to discuss how it could raise that quantity, and from those discussions it developed a goal to double the number of patients served from 21 million in 2011 to 40 million in 2020 (Novo Nordisk 2015a; Black Sun Pic and IIRC 2014).

So how do we compare Novo Nordisk's results to that of other companies? Since it is not reporting to a standardized framework such as GRI, how can we be assured that it is following appropriate reporting standards? Fortunately, there are numerous other standards the company has used, some of which you will recognize (CSRWire 2015):

- International Financial Reporting Standards (IFRS)
- Danish Financial Statements Act
- Reference to the content elements and guiding principles of the International Integrated Reporting Council's IR draft framework
- The accountability standard, the AA1000 (2008) Framework, which includes AA1000APS (2008) and AA1000AS (2008)
- U.S. Sarbanes-Oxley Act requirements for financial reporting

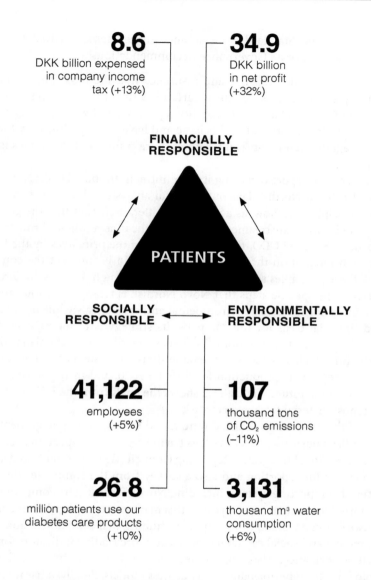

Figure 13.1 The triple bottom line (Novo Nordisk 2015a)

- International Standards on Assurance Engagements (ISAE) 3000
- Danish Corporate Governance Recommendations

These help to provide credence and assurance that the most important and material topics are addressed. This is certainly a time of continuing transition in the field of financial and sustainability reporting, and we felt it was important for you to be introduced to this issue and have some preliminary tools to analyze integrated reporting as it becomes more commonplace in the sustainability world.

In the separate report regarding its commitment to the UNGC (Novo Nordisk 2015b), Novo Nordisk lays out a careful analysis of how it is committed to these principles and how, as a practical matter, it ensures that the goals are implemented and mainstreamed into the business as a whole. From a clear commitment from the CEO, through adoption of the principles by the board, and through integration throughout the business, it is apparent the company is taking these principles seriously. On pages 27 through 35 of its 2015 report, it reports on the specific steps that Novo Nordisk is taking in various areas to improve its performance on environmental and social goals while maintaining a sound financial basis for the company. Its strategy is to leverage synergies between the various triple-bottom-line issues to strike the best balance of risk and opportunity. This includes setting ambitious goals, such as 100 percent renewable energy for its production facilities by 2020, and incorporating Scope 3 emissions in the future. Figure 13.2 shows the goals from the UNGC that are deemed most material for Novo Nordisk.

Most of the material goals listed were found to be in strong alignment with Novo Nordisk's business goals as well as having a positive impact on society.

The International Integrated Reporting Council (IIRC) has published an initial framework for reporting and also a survey from the companies that have embraced this reporting system, including Novo Nordisk. The companies that have reported for more than one year in this manner have seen a better connection between financial and other capitals—finding that the information about environmental and social capital has provided more leading indicators for their financial performance. Also, this connectivity has helped to improve their insight into long-term performance and business models. Finally, it has improved internal decision processes by connecting the value creation of the capital investment in sustainability (Black Sun Pic and IIRC 2014).

The GRI is working on a framework for integrated reporting and is in the process of convening experts to develop the appropriate planning process. Its perspective is that integrative reporting is driven by integrative thinking, showing the deeper connections between stakeholder groups and financial reporting. It should not result in just one report. Rather, its goal is that an integrated

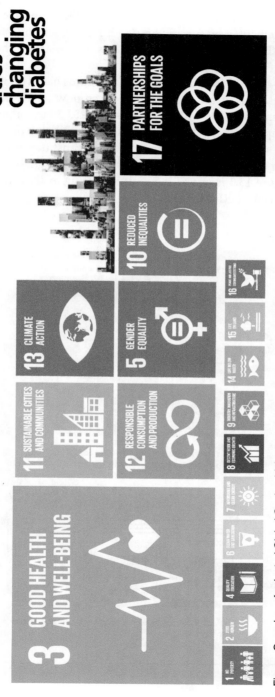

Figure: Overview of selected Global Goals which are most material for Novo Nordisk in terms of a possible positive impact on society in strong alignment with business goals. All Global Goals and the targets related to each of them will be a part of an overall assessment to be carried out in 2016 on how Novo Nordisk could contribute to their fulfilment.

Figure 13.2 Novo Nordisk Material Goals (Novo Nordisk 2015b)

report may provide an overall summary showing the links and feedback and that it can be supplemented by specific, in-depth reports serving various constituencies. Watch this space as the GRI continues to investigate and convene experts in this area (GRI 2016a).

In October 2016 the GRI issued a new set of standards based on its previous reporting guidelines. This means that companies can now certify their reporting to this set of standards. The GRI says this is not GRI 5 but rather is a more disciplined way to approach its reporting. The standard is based on the GRI G4 guidelines but with some editing and clarification. The institute also provides a mapping document to coordinate reporting between the G4 guidelines and the new standards. Figure 13.3 is one of the tools it is using to show the relationships among the various GRI standards.

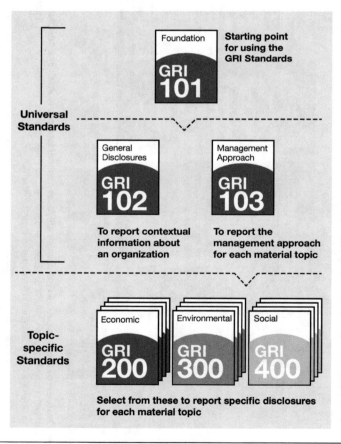

Figure 13.3   The New GRI Standards (GRI 2016b)

I have provided links to the updated GRI Standards at the end of this chapter. This will be an area of investigation for companies around the world. The sand seems to be continually shifting regarding how to report on sustainability and the choice of the GRI versus the Sustainability Accounting Standards Board versus the IIRC will continue. The good news is that this debate drives transparency and stakeholder engagement, and all seem to have in common the desire for the most material aspects to be reported on. That is also good news for our field and for responsible business management.

I invite you to investigate Novo Nordisk. The company has experienced significant growth over the past decade, yet appears not to have lost its focus on their main goals and core values, including the goal to improve human health globally and provide affordable access to its medications.

ADDITIONAL RESOURCES

How to Read a Corporate Social Responsibility Report (Boston College)

Boston College has published a number of top-quality white papers. This report provides background on CSR reporting in general, as well as tips for sorting the greenwashing from the truly valuable data in a CSR report. It is available at:

- https://iri.hks.harvard.edu/files/iri/files/how_to_read_a_corporate_social _responsibility_report.pdf.

Value of Social Reporting (Boston College)

Here is another helpful white paper from Boston College—this time helping a company build the business case for a CSR. It can be accessed at:

- http://iri.hks.harvard.edu/files/iri/files/value-of-social-reporting.pdf.

KPMG International Survey of Corporate Responsibility Reporting

KPMG publishes annual updates to these surveys. In its 2017 survey, KPMG found that 78 percent of the world's 250 largest corporations integrate non-financial data into their financial reporting, a growing trend in the industry. The trend toward third-party audits is also increasing—to a total of 65 percent in 2017 for larger companies. The 2017 report highlights financial risks to climate change and linking reporting to the UN Sustainable Development goals. It is available at:

- https://home.kpmg.com/content/dam/kpmg/campaigns/csr/pdf/CSR _Reporting_2017.pdf.

HBR: Leadership in the Age of Transparency

This article was mentioned in Chapter 3, but it is worth mentioning again in case you missed it. Taking ownership of the externalities of a business and reporting on them in a transparent manner can be the best approach to avoiding risks that will negatively impact the business in the long run. You can access this article at:

- https://hbr.org/2010/04/the-big-idea-leadership-in-the-age-of-trans parency.

Bob Willard and Maureen Hart are leading sustainability professionals. In the article—"Are We There Yet? Bringing a New Framework to Sustainability"—they promote two new reporting tools that improve company internal performance: the S-CORE™ Sustainability Assessment and Future Fit Business Benchmark. It is available at:

- https://www.triplepundit.com/story/2014/are-we-there-yet-bringing -new-framework-sustainability/39836.

ADDITIONAL CASE RESOURCES

Novo Nordisk Annual Report

Novo Nordisk has been filing integrated financial and sustainability reports for the past decade. You'll find downloadable versions of its annual report as well as a separate corporate governance report at this link:

- https://www.novonordisk.com/annual-report.html.

Novo Nordisk: UNGC Communication on Progress 2017

This link takes you to information on how Novo Nordisk has progressed on the UNGC and Sustainable Development goals. It is listed as being qualified for the Global Compact Advanced Level. You can find it at:

- https://www.unglobalcompact.org/participation/report/cop/create-and -submit/advanced/414321.

International Integrated Reporting Framework

The document listed here outlines the fundamental concepts, guiding principles, and content elements for integrative reporting. Rather than prescriptive specific key performance indicators, it describes how an integrated report is assembled and how it should relate to the outside forces and future value of a corporation. It is available at:

- http://integratedreporting.org/resource/international-ir-framework/.

Introducing the New GRI Standards

This link provides information on the new GRI Standards, including a video introduction to the new standards and how they will link to the earlier GRI G4 Reporting Guidelines. The standards must be used by July 2018 for those reporting with the GRI Framework. They can be found at:

- https://www.globalreporting.org/standards/getting-started-with-the-gri -standards/.

QUESTIONS FOR THIS CHAPTER

1. *Materiality*: Even as materiality is important in GRI reporting, it is also one of the essential issues for integrated reporting. What are some of the material issues that Novo Nordisk is reporting on, and why are they important? How is it connecting these issues to the other data points in its business?

2. *Human progress*: What are some of the most important areas of social progress for Novo Nordisk? What are the metrics it is using to report on these issues? How is it relating its performance to financial reporting? Are there environmental connections to its social progress as well?

3. *Environmental progress*: What are some of the most important areas of environmental progress for Novo Nordisk? Are there specific problem areas the company recognizes? What are the metrics it is using to report on these issues? How is it relating its progress here to financial reporting? Are there social connections to its environmental concerns as well?

4. *Economic progress*: What are the key financial reporting areas for Novo Nordisk, and how does the company relate these issues to its environmental and social issues? What are the metrics it is using to report on these issues? How is the company relating its financial progress to the

outside forces in the business world? What are the key risks and opportunities it recognizes and how is it planning for these?

REFERENCES

Biesener, S. (September–October 2011). "Connecting the Dots: At Novo Nordisk
and Elsewhere, Integrated Reporting Presents the Value A Company
Creates in Ways That Are Not Captured on a Balance Sheet." *Communication
World, 28*(5). Retrieved from: https://www.questia.com/magazine/1G1
-265373174/connecting-the-dots-at-novo-nordisk-and-elsewhere.
Black Sun Pic and the IIRC. (2014). "The Integrated Reporting journey: The
inside story." London: Black Sun Pic and the IIRC. Retrieved from: http://
integratedreporting.org/wp-content/uploads/2015/07/The-Integrated
-Reporting-journey-the-inside-story.pdf.
Corporate Knights. (2016). "2016 Global 100 Results." Retrieved from: http://
www.corporateknights.com/magazines/2016-global-100-issue/2016
-global-100-results-14533333/.
CSRWire. (2015). "Novo Nordisk Publishes 2014 Integrated Annual Report
Emphasizing Long-Term Thinking." CSRWire, LLC. Retrieved from:
http://www.csrwire.com/press_releases/37668-Novo-Nordisk-Publishes
-2014-Integrated-Annual-Report-Emphasising-Long-Term-Thinking.
Forbes. (2018). "The World's Largest Public Companies." Retrieved from:
https://www.forbes.com/global2000/list/#search:Novo%20Nordisk.
Global Reporting Initiative (GRI). (2016a). "Forging a Path to Integrated Re-
porting." Amsterdam, Netherlands: GRI. Retrieved from: https://www
.globalreporting.org/resourcelibrary/GRI-CLG_IntegratedReporting.pdf.
Global Reporting Initiative (GRI). (2016b). "Consolidated Set of GRI Sus-
tainability Reporting Standards 2016." Amsterdam, Netherlands: GRI.
Retrieved from: https://www.globalreporting.org/standards/gri-standards
-download-center/.
Novo Nordisk. (2012). "Global Reporting Initiative 2012." Bagsværd, Denmark:
Novo Nordisk. Retrieved from: http://www.novonordisk.com/content/
dam/Denmark/HQ/Commons/documents/Novo-Nordisk-Global
-Reporting-Initiative-2012.pdf.
Novo Nordisk. (2014). "Novo Nordisk Annual Report." Bagsværd, Denmark:
Novo Nordisk. Retrieved from: http://www.novonordisk.com/content/dam/
Denmark/HQ/Commons/documents/Novo-Nordisk-Annual-Report
-2014.pdf.

Novo Nordisk. (2015a). "Novo Nordisk Annual Report 2015." Bagsværd, Denmark: Novo Nordisk. Retrieved from: http://www.novonordisk.com/content/dam/Denmark/HQ/Commons/documents/Novo-Nordisk-Annual-Report-2015.pdf.

Novo Nordisk. (2015b). "United Nations Global Compact Communication on Progress." Bagsværd, Denmark: Novo Nordisk. Retrieved from: http://www.novonordisk.com/content/dam/Denmark/HQ/Commons/documents/Novo-Nordisk-UN-Global-Compact-2015.pdf.

Novo Nordisk. (2017). "Novo Nordisk Annual Report 2017." Bagsværd, Denmark: Novo Nordisk. Retrieved from: https://www.novonordisk.com/content/dam/Denmark/HQ/investors/irmaterial/annual_report/2018/NN-AR17_UK_Online1.pdf.

CHAPTER 14

SUSTAINABLE DESIGN AT JONES LANG LASALLE

With this chapter's focus on design, marketing, and stewardship, here is an opportunity to look at the built environment and how these elements of sustainability can reduce society's impact on resources as well as improve productivity and social well-being. Our cases so far in this book have taken you to various areas of manufacturing, retail, resource extraction and refining, and pharmaceuticals. These industries all utilize commercial buildings, and so the design and operation of these buildings can have an important impact on the world's resources and the people who occupy those buildings. Buildings are responsible for roughly 40 percent of the world's greenhouse gas (GHG) emissions, so improving the energy efficiency of these buildings can significantly contribute to reducing overall emissions. Jones Lang LaSalle (JLL) has long been a leader in this area, and now controls over 4 billion square feet of real estate globally for its various clients. In 2017 it had revenues of $7.9 billion, ranking the company number 391 on the Fortune 500 and was named by Fortune as one of the Most Admired Companies in 2017 (JLL 2017a).

In 2016 it was invited to participate in the World Green Building Council's Advisory Board, furthering its mission to enable green building through business and market transformations. By facilitating green building practices with its clients, JLL is leveraging its expertise to reduce the energy footprint of businesses around the world (WorldGBC 2016; JLL 2016).

JLL has a long list of sustainability, governance, and ethics awards. Part of this emphasis resulted from the acquisition of companies possessing that expertise over the past decade, including Upstream, a leading sustainability consultancy in the United Kingdom. We have mentioned how such acquisitions can help inform the acquiring company as well as provide resources to the company being acquired. Past examples have included Unilever's acquisition of Ben & Jerry's, Clorox's purchase of Burt's Bees, and VF Corporation's purchase of Timberland. For JLL, growth through merger and acquisition appears to be part of its business plan ever since the merger of JLW and LaSalle Partners in 1999, making JLL the world's leading real estate management and investment firm (JLL 2015a).

JLL's sustainability report for 2013 was a honed-down version from previous efforts (at 20 pages versus 44 pages for the 2012 report). JLL stated that it decided to focus its reporting on fewer items after conducting a materiality review in early 2014 (JLL 2013). You will remember a similar result from Marks & Spencer, reducing its reported items from 180 in 2012 to 100 in 2013. JLL promised a more complete analysis of its data for 2016 on its website at the end of the year, and that has surfaced. Its 2016 sustainability report also has an index at the end organized along the GRI G4 Guidelines. For your background research, you can find the earlier sustainability reports on the JLL website.

The report for 2017 states that it has met all its previous targets, and this report sets new goals based on the UN Sustainable Development goals (SDGs) that are most material to JLL. Figure 14.1 shows the selected goals and their descriptions (JLL 2017b).

3: Good health and well-being
Ensure healthy lives and promote well-being for all at all ages.

5: Gender equality
Achieve gender equality and empower all women and girls.

8: Decent work and economic growth
Promote sustained, inclusive, and sustainable economic growth, full and productive employment, and decent work for all.

11: Sustainable cities and communities
Make cities and human settlements inclusive, safe, resilient, and sustainable.

12: Responsible consumption & production
Ensure sustainable consumption and production patterns.

13: Climate action
Take urgent action to combat climate change and its impacts.

Figure 14.1   Most material SDGs for JLL (JLL 2017b)

As JLL's sustainability reports profess, the business of saving clients money on energy and building maintenance is a core strategy of the company. It has developed detailed databases of building information to help inform clients about the various choices available for new construction, leasing, and remodeling. Providing this expertise can have a significant effect on the future impacts of commercial space.

Indeed, in a report by Architecture 2030 (2017), the U.S. building sector is on track to meet the goals set out by the Paris Accord's reduction targets. This means that current trends predict reducing consumption by 24.5 percent below 2005 levels by 2020 and to 30.4 percent by 2030. This is encouraging news and speaks to the work of companies like JLL gaining ground in the marketplace. Figures 14.2A–C show graphs indicating the revised estimates.

Reporting on its own incremental success can be challenging in the commercial real estate business, however. As the 2013 JLL report shows, the metrics from year to year can vary depending on the timing of completion of long-term projects. The numbers for 2013 show a significant dip, and the report notes that some of this is due to projects coming on line that are not yet complete, in spite of a 33 percent increase in projects for the company. It also notes that more long-term client relationships mean that the easy solutions may have already been found and that digging deeper for cost savings may result in slower returns on investment. Yet it also notes that improving the energy efficiency of a building can yield improvements in overall comfort and environment for those

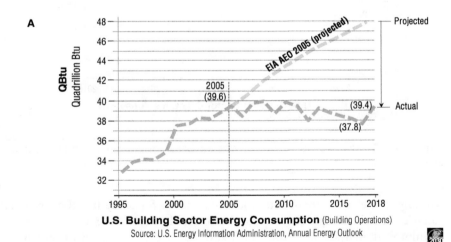

Figure 14.2A   Building sector projections for GHG emissions (Architecture 2030, 2017)

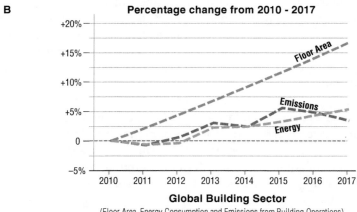

Figure 14.2B   Building sector projections for GHG emissions (Architecture 2030, 2017)

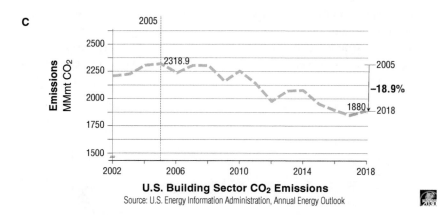

Figure 14.2C   Building sector projections for GHG emissions (Architecture 2030, 2017)

working in the space. Increased productivity levels for office-based operations can mean marked improvements for the bottom line (JLL 2013).

Improved analysis and projections have enabled JLL to meet its targets in recent years, and having achieved all its targets in 2017, JLL set new, ambitious goals for future years. It now has targets to align with the Paris Accord and measurements based on scientific analysis for climate change (JLL 2017b).

On the social side, JLL attests to a relentless focus on ethical standards. Its commitment to excellent service requires a commitment to integrity, technological expertise, and thought leadership. The company's involvement with leading nongovernmental organizations such as the Carbon Disclosure Project, World Green Building Council, Ethisphere Institute, and the Boston College Center for Corporate Citizenship helps to inform its practice and increase its reach. JLL has received recognition for its work, including a perfect score by the Human Rights Campaign Foundation's Corporate Equality Index, and was rated first in the financial services/real estate/insurance sector for *CR Magazine's* 100 Best Corporate Citizens (JLL 2013; JLL 2017b).

The supply chain for JLL is different than that of a typical manufacturing company, yet its choices for procurement affect an enormous platform of suppliers, from building materials to janitorial service companies. JLL's policies in this regard can therefore have a significant impact on energy use, resources consumed, and the welfare of the workforce. How are its policies defined? How does the company influence its clients? What kinds of policies and practices is it able to project? These are a few of the questions you will investigate in this chapter as you delve into JLL and its spheres of influence.

ADDITIONAL RESOURCES

Living Building Challenge

The Living Building Challenge incorporates seven *petals* into its certification process: place, water, energy, health and happiness, materials, equity, and beauty. They can be adapted to various scales and designs for buildings, and the certification aims provide the most sustainable measures for the built environment, providing a regenerative environmental impact. For more information see:

- https://living-future.org/lbc/.

U.S. Green Building Council (USGBC)

Once a challenging idea in green building, the USGBC's LEED certifications are now widely used in all types of building construction. This link to its website opens the door to its various standards:

- http://www.usgbc.org/leed.

Rocky Mountain Institute (RMI): Big Pipes Small Pumps (2011)

This white paper from the RMI describes how multiple benefits can result from simple design changes and how predicting those outcomes can help to provide the business case to invest in those changes. It is available at:

- https://d231jw5ce53gcq.cloudfront.net/wp-content/uploads/2017/04/OCS_BigPipes_SmallPumps_Interface_2011.pdf.

ADDITIONAL CASE RESOURCES

JLL Reports

Beginning in 2015, JLL published its first integrated report according to the principles of the Integrated Reporting (IR) Framework. It also publishes separate sustainability reports and governance reports. You can download the latest report and previous sustainability and annual reports for JLL at its Investor Relations webpage:

- http://ir.jll.com/phoenix.zhtml?c=81245&p=irol-IRHome.

Empire State Building Overview

JLL was one of the partners turning a major planned retrofit of the Empire State Building with zero percent energy savings into a deep retrofit that saved 38 percent in annual energy costs. This document describes the role of the various partners and the design process:

- http://www.esbnyc.com/sites/default/files/ESBOverviewDeck.pdf.

You can also find additional information about the Empire State Building retrofit at:

- http://www.esbnyc.com/esb-sustainability/press-and-resources.

QUESTIONS FOR THIS CHAPTER

1. *Design—climate and energy*: How is JLL influencing the design of new and existing buildings to improve their energy and resource efficiency?

How is the company making a difference in the operation of existing buildings? How is it making the business case for clients to invest in green building practices for owned or leased space? What are some of the major challenges it faces in making improvements in this area? You also might like to take a look at the Empire State Building remodel project that is included in the case reading folder. What impact did JLL have on this project?

2. *Marketing—community and supply chain*: How does JLL provide for guidelines in its supply chain beyond its code of conduct? How is the company impacting communities around the world with its various procurement decisions or recommendations? Is there more it could do to influence its suppliers based on the other companies presented in this book?

3. *Stewardship—global diversity*: JLL appears to be a leader in diversity in its workforce. How does the company compare with other global companies? How has it set and achieved these goals? How does a more diverse workforce and leadership team improve stewardship responsibility for JLL?

REFERENCES

Architecture 2030. (2017). "On Track to Meet the Paris Agreement." Architecture 2030. Retrieved from: http://architecture2030.org/on-track-to-meet-the-paris-agreement/.

JLL. (2013). "2013 Sustainability Report: We Are JLL. We Take Responsibility." Chicago, IL: Jones Lang LaSalle Incorporated. Retrieved from: http://www.jll.com/Documents/csr/JLL-2013-Sustainability-Report.pdf.

JLL. (2015a). "A Tale of Two Cities and Global Expansion." Chicago, IL: Jones Lang LaSalle Incorporated. Retrieved from: http://www.jll.com/about/our-history.

JLL. (2015b). "Our Cities. Our Future." 2014 Global Sustainability Report. Chicago, IL: Jones Lang LaSalle Incorporated. Retrieved from: http://www.jll.com/sustainability/sustainability-report.

JLL. (2016). "Building a Better Tomorrow." 2016 Global Sustainability Report. Chicago, IL: Jones Lang LaSalle Incorporated. Retrieved from: http://www.jll.com/Documents/csr/JLL-2015-Global-Sustainability-Report.pdf.

JLL. (2017a). "JLL among biggest movers up Fortune 500." Chicago, IL: Jones Lang LaSalle Incorporated. Retrieved from: http://www.jll.com/news/304/jll-among-biggest-movers-up-fortune-500.

JLL. (2017b). "Building a Better Tomorrow: Our Sustainability Leadership Ambition" JLL Sustainability Report. Chicago, IL: Jones Lang LaSalle Incorporated. Retrieved from: http://www.jll.com/Documents/csr/JLL -2017-Global-Sustainability-Report.pdf.

WorldGBC. (2016). "JLL joins WorldGBC's global advisory board." Toronto, Canada: World Green Building Council. Retrieved from: https://www.worldgbc.org/news-media/jll-joins-worldgbc%E2%80%99s -corporate-advisory-board.

CHAPTER 15

CONCLUSION: INNOVATION AND SUSTAINABILITY

In our final chapter of case material, we investigate innovation. A popular topic in business schools, it is now being linked to sustainability as well as profitability. Most of the literature in this area focuses on product innovation, but it is also important to think about innovation as it applies to processes and business models. In this way, innovation can improve a company's sustainability without necessarily increasing consumption.

Although there is no single case for this chapter, I offer a few ideas about companies that have been particularly innovative in sustainability or social marketing. I also invite you to investigate your own ideas; think about which companies you admire and why. The journey to sustainability is a winding one, and not every company succeeds in every way, but many offer examples that can be replicated and spread among peers and competitors. I encourage you to do your best to facilitate this transfer of knowledge for a better world.

CASE COMPANIES FOR INNOVATION

During the 1990s, Nike suffered from protests and boycotts after poor labor conditions were exposed in its Southeast Asia factories. It took almost a decade for Nike to take the problem seriously, but in the early 2000s they began working with other companies to improve worker conditions, and today they are a leader in sustainability throughout their operations and distribution chain. Innovation has been a major component in their success, from materials use to factory design. Their social policies have resulted in more women in leadership positions and featuring women athletes in the 2016 Olympics. You can find more information regarding Nike's sustainability policies at:

- https://sustainability.nike.com/.

BrasKam is a petrochemical company that is highly rated for its sustainability and innovation practices. It is listed on the Dow Jones Sustainability Index and also rated *A* by the Carbon Disclosure Project. It is developing plastics made from sugar cane, and is researching safer chemical substitutes for chlorine and other toxic ingredients in its supply chain. You can find more information regarding BrasKam's innovation and sustainability at:

- https://www.braskem.com.br/usa/innovation-and-sustainability.

Sanergy is not a multinational corporation. Rather, it is a small start-up founded by two graduate students from MIT. They provide low-cost, hygienic toilets in Africa where urban environments have little or no sanitation facilities. Their business model uses local franchises to service the units and convert the waste to fertilizer and biogas. They are supported by the Bill and Melinda Gates Foundation and as of 2018 have operations in Kenya. You can find more information about Sanergy at:

- http://www.sanergy.com/.

These two companies have already been mentioned in this book as exemplars, but it is worth listing them here again since they are also recognized for their innovative practices: Levi Strauss for its recycling of old product into new and for using recycled plastic bottles in some of their fabrics and Patagonia for starting its own venture fund to encourage more research in sustainable solutions for water, energy, food, clothing, and waste. You can access more information regarding these companies at:

- https://levistrauss.com/sustainability/products/wasteless/.
- http://www.tinshedventures.com/.

Cofounded by Sir Richard Branson and Jochen Zeitz in 2012, The B Team's purpose is to bring business leaders together to further the well-being of people and the planet and to leverage business leadership to effect meaningful change for a sustainable future. Information about The B Team can be accessed at:

- http://bteam.org.

The WeSpire Employee Engagement Company is an innovative company that works with large corporations to engage their employees in sustainable lifestyles and drive positive impact throughout the organization. For more information, you can go to:

- http://www.wespire.com.

ADDITIONAL RESOURCES

This article describes research showing a strong causal correlation between sustainability and the ability to innovate. Sustainability can drive innovation because it forces businesses to look at problems in a different way—by solving for emissions, for example, or resolving supply chain issues from an environmental or social perspective. For more information, check online for:

- Deloitte. (2013). "Sustainability-Driven Innovation."

The authors argue that modern corporations are missing the boat (and cost savings) if they don't have sustainability at the core of their business. For more information, check online for:

- *Harvard Business Review.* (2009). "Why Sustainability Is Now the Key Driver of Innovation."

Sustainability can provide the kind of disruptive change to get a business out of its comfort zone and into innovative transformations. For more information, check online for:

- Harvard Business School. (2007). "Jumpstarting Innovation: Using Disruption to Your Advantage."

RECOMMENDED BOOKS

Christensen, C. M. (2011). *The Innovator's Dilemma: The Revolutionary Book That Will Change the Way You Do Business.* New York, NY: HarperBusiness.

Isaacson, W. (2015). *The Innovators: How a Group of Hackers, Geniuses, and Geeks Created the Digital Revolution.* New York, NY: Simon & Schuster.

Lovins, A. and Rocky Mountain Institute. (2011). *Reinventing Fire: Bold Business Solutions for the New Energy Era.* Hartford, CT: Chelsea Green Publishing.

APPENDIX **1.1**

UN GLOBAL COMPACT: TEN PRINCIPLES FOR SUSTAINABILITY

HUMAN RIGHTS

Principle 1: Businesses should support and respect the protection of internationally proclaimed human rights; and

Principle 2: make sure that they are not complicit in human rights abuses.

LABOUR

Principle 3: Businesses should uphold the freedom of association and the effective recognition of the right to collective bargaining;

Principle 4: the elimination of all forms of forced and compulsory labour;

Principle 5: the effective abolition of child labour; and

Principle 6: the elimination of discrimination in respect of employment and occupation.

ENVIRONMENT

Principle 7: Businesses should support a precautionary approach to environmental challenges;

Principle 8: undertake initiatives to promote greater environmental responsibility; and

Principle 9: encourage the development and diffusion of environmentally friendly technologies.

ANTI-CORRUPTION

Principle 10: Businesses should work against corruption in all its forms, including extortion and bribery.

An explanation of each of these principles and the background for the development of these principles is available at the UN Global Compact website: https://www.unglobalcompact .org/what-is-gc/mission/principles.

CR MAGAZINE: TOP 10 OF THE 100 BEST CORPORATE CITIZENS, 2019

Every year, *CR Magazine* publishes a list of companies it considers to be the best corporate citizens. Go to the link listed here to view the entire list and learn about their methodology.

Rank	Company	Symbol	Overall Weighted Score	Employee Relations	Environment	Climate Change	Stakeholders and Society	Human Rights	ISS-ESG Corporate Rank	Governance	Financial
1	Owens Corning	OC	84.97	42	47	31	6	1	1	346	116
2	Intel Corp.	INTC	83.32	4	5	13	7	65	2	704	8
3	General Mills, Inc.	GIS	82.72	30	84	9	9	13	95	466	65
4	Campbell Soup Co.	CPB	80.84	143	36	101	11	12	96	34	110
5	HP, Inc.	HPQ	80.69	41	71	1	41	76	97	35	140
6	Microsoft Corp.	MSFT	80.09	114	65	162	3	10	98	99	19
7	Nielsen Holdings PLC	NLSN	79.91	29	30	308	15	4	3	36	795
8	Ecolab, Inc.	ECL	79.81	18	24	153	58	9	57	347	658
9	Gap, Inc.	GPS	78.01	16	49	140	80	11	151	194	762
10	Cisco Systems, Inc.	CSCO	77.22	100	50	32	49	41	41	348	372

CR Magazine. (2019). 100 best corporate citizens, 20th anniversary. Northampton, MA: CR Magazine. Retrieved from: https://www.3blassociation.com/files/yMblCg/100BestCorporate Citizens_2019.pdf.

APPENDIX **2.1**

EIGHT KEY LESSONS FROM EIGHT YEARS OF SURVEYS: *MIT SLOAN MANAGEMENT REVIEW*

Key Lesson #1: Set your sustainability vision and ambition: 90% of executives see sustainability as important, but only 60% of companies have a sustainability strategy.

Key Lesson #2: Focus on material issues: Companies that focus on material issues report up to 50% added profit from sustainability. Those that don't focus on their material issues struggle to add value from their sustainability activities.

Key Lesson #3: Set up the right organization to achieve your ambition: Building sustainability into business units doubles an organization's chance of profiting from its sustainability activities.

Key Lesson #4: Explore business model innovation opportunities: Nearly 50% of companies have changed their business models as a result of sustainability opportunities.

Key Lesson #5: Develop a clear business case for sustainability: While 60% of companies have a sustainability strategy, only 25% have developed a clear business case for their sustainability efforts.

Key Lesson #6: Get the board of directors on board: 86% of respondents agreed that boards should play a strong role in their company's sustainability efforts, but only 48% say their CEOs are engaged, and fewer (30%) agreed that their sustainability efforts had strong board-level oversight.

Key Lesson #7: Develop a compelling sustainability value creation story for investors: 75% of executives in investment companies think sustainability performance should be considered in investment decisions, but only 60% of corporate executives think investors care about sustainability performance.

Key Lesson #8: Collaborate with a variety of stakeholders to drive strategic change: 90% of executives believe collaboration is essential to sustainability success, but only 47% say their companies collaborate strategically.

MIT Sloan Management Review and The Boston Consulting Group. (2017). "Corporate Sustainability at a Crossroads." Cambridge, MA: Massachusetts Institute of Technology. Available from: https://sloanreview.mit.edu/projects/corporate-sustainability-at-a-crossroads/.

SHARED VALUE IN BRIEF
(PORTER AND KRAMER)

The concept of shared value—which focuses on the connections between societal and economic progress—has the power to unleash the next wave of global growth.

An increasing number of companies known for their hard-nosed approach to business—such as Google, IBM, Intel, Johnson & Johnson, Nestlé, Unilever, and Wal-Mart—have begun to embark on important shared value initiatives. But our understanding of the potential of shared value is just beginning.

There are three key ways that companies can create shared value opportunities:

- By re-conceiving products and markets
- By redefining productivity in the value chain
- By enabling local cluster development

Every firm should look at decisions and opportunities through the lens of shared value. This will lead to new approaches that generate greater innovation and growth for companies—and also greater benefits for society.

Porter M. and M. Kramer. (2011). "Creating Shared Value": https://hbr.org/2011/01/the-big -idea-creating-shared-value.

PROJECT SIGMA: BUSINESS CASE TOOL

BUILDING A BUSINESS CASE—THE PROCESS

The following five steps provide a simple process for developing a tailored business case. They are a guide only and should be used as necessary in developing your own business case.

1. Understand Your Significant Impacts

Understand the organization's significant impacts on the environment, society, and the economy and what opportunities and risks they represent. There are many tools available to carry out appraisals, for an example see the SIGMA Opportunity and Risk Guide. The most obvious impacts, detailed in existing information, may well be the most significant and offer a good starting point, however a systematic assessment across the full range of organizational activities provides greater confidence that all impacts will be identified.

2. Identify Key Stakeholders' Issues

Remember that the management of perceptions is as important as the management of actual impacts and will influence organizational ability to maximize opportunities and minimize risks. Consulting stakeholders on what they consider to be the key sustainable development impacts of an organization will significantly strengthen the business case. The SIGMA Stakeholder Engagement Tool, for example, can be used to do this.

3. Make It Relevant

Link the opportunities and risks identified in Steps 1 and 2 above to core business. If your organization has a business plan or key strategic objectives, map the issues and impacts to them. Use a style and language that is easily understandable to the intended audience—e.g., follow the language and style of the business plan. This ensures that any business case is fully aligned to the core purpose of the organization and will enhance the credibility of the business case.

4.   Back It Up

Provide examples, data, and supporting information for each opportunity or risk, both from outside and within the organization. In particular, wherever financial costs and benefits can be calculated or are available, include them.

5.   Keep It Dynamic and Updated

Ensure the business case is dynamic and develops as organizational priorities, sustainable development understanding, and best practices change. A considered and up-to-date business case helps communicate and raise awareness of the strengths and weaknesses of improved sustainable development management and keeps it relevant for its intended audiences.

SIGMA. (2003). *The SIGMA Guidelines—Toolkit: SIGMA Business Case Tool.* London, UK: AccountAbility, BSI, Forum for the Future.

Project SIGMA created a number of helpful guides for sustainability practice. The SIGMA Business Case Tool was published in 2003. Unfortunately, their website is unavailable as of this publication. I am providing parts of the tool here for your reference and use. From this document, here is an explanation of Project Sigma:

About the SIGMA Project

The SIGMA Project, *Sustainability Integrated Guidelines for Management*, was launched in 1999 with the support of the UK Department of Trade and Industry (DTI) and is led by:

- British Standards Institution: the leading standards organization
- Forum for the Future: a leading sustainability charity and think tank
- AccountAbility: the international professional body for accountability

The SIGMA project has developed the SIGMA Guidelines and a series of tools to provide clear, practical advice to organizations to enable them to make a meaningful contribution to sustainable development.

SIGMA. (2003). *The SIGMA Guidelines—Toolkit: SIGMA Business Case Tool.* London, UK: AccountAbility, BSI, Forum for the Future.

APPENDIX **2.4**

SIGMA GUIDELINES: BUSINESS BENEFITS TO SUSTAINABILITY

Improved operational efficiency	Preservation of license to operate
Enhanced brand value and reputation	Promoting and increasing innovation
Customer attraction and retention	Improved access to capital
Enhanced human and intellectual capital	Building and sustaining shareholder value
Improved management of risk	Generating increased revenues
Attracting and retaining talented staff	Identification of new opportunities

SIGMA Project. (2003). *The SIGMA Guidelines: Putting Sustainable Development into Practice—A Guide for Organizations.* London, UK: BSI.

PATAGONIA FOOTPRINT CHRONICLES©: MADE IN CHINA

WHERE WE MAKE OUR PRODUCTS AND WHY

In this document we hope to address your questions about where we make our products and why. It's a complicated subject, but we'll do our best to provide our views.

WE DON'T OWN FARMS, MILLS OR FACTORIES

Like most clothing companies these days, Patagonia doesn't own the farms, fabric mills or cut and sew factories that contribute to the production of our products. Yet what is done in our name is not invisible to us. We are responsible for all the workers who make our goods and for all that goes into a piece of clothing that bears a Patagonia label. It took us a long time to ask ourselves what we owe people who work for others in our supply chain. We had high sewing standards, even for casual sportswear, and exacting standards for technical clothes. To meet quality requirements, our production staff had always been drawn to clean, well-lighted factories that employed experienced sewing operators. Although we had always bargained with our factories over price and terms, we never chased lowest-cost labor.

QUALITY IS OUR PRINCIPLE CRITERION FOR SOURCING

Quality is our principle criterion for selecting a supplier; cost becomes a subset. That is, given the choice between two factories that meet our required level of quality and specific performance characteristics, we might opt for the one with the lower rice—if we know we can trust the lower-cost source. This is true of all sourcing decisions from fiber choice to fabric construction to sewing. Reduced environmental harm is a strong second criterion. If we can reduce environmental harm without sacrificing quality we do so; where reduced harm will increase the price, we make judgment calls; the environment often wins, even when we think a decision will cost us sales.

FAIR TREATMENT OF WORKERS

We're committed to working in factories that treat well the workers who make Patagonia goods, and we do many things to try to ensure that outcome. These include an in-house Social and Environmental Responsibility staff guided by our Workplace Code of Conduct and matching benchmark document, active membership with the Fair Labor Association and International Labor Organization, factory audits for social compliance and more.[1] Such a commitment can sometimes raise the cost of our products made anywhere in Asia, as well as the rest of the world. But to us, it's time and money well spent.

QUALIFIED AMERICAN FACTORIES ARE TOUGH TO FIND

During our early years we sourced at least half our products outside the U.S. But our percentage of American-made products has decreased over time, as has the U.S. textile industry and the number of domestic high-quality sewing shops. Much of the U.S. apparel manufacturing landscape simply no longer exists. Seattle contractors Cascade, J&E, and Down Products are no longer in business. Pyke Manufacturing of Utah declared chapter 11 in 1994, and Tennessee Apparel, Everite of Pennsylvania, and Linda Apparel of San Francisco have long since shut their doors. It is very difficult for clothing companies to find factories in the U.S. that meet our standards. The textile industry is much smaller; the work has shifted overseas.

The shrinking textile industry in the United States is due in large part to trade agreements, including NAFTA (duty free with Mexico & Canada), CAFTA (duty free with Central American countries), ATPA (duty free with Colombia

[1] For a full account, go to this link: https://www.patagonia.com/working-with-factories.html.

and other Andean countries), and IFTA (duty free from Israel). These trade agreements have directly contributed to the dramatic decline in the U.S.-based textile and sewn product industries since 1994. Patagonia fought NAFTA and paid for ads in *The New York Times* and other newspapers around the county in opposition to the NAFTA treaty because we feared it would degrade environmental standards and because it would displace American workers.

We are always searching to find high-quality, U.S.-based manufacturing options but, in our experience, the options are very limited. Trade programs that have encouraged textile and sewing manufacturers to move offshore have meant that the factories that remain have a difficult time providing the capacity we need. The number of sewing workers required to produce tens of thousands of garments each season, many of which are very complex, are extremely hard to find. We continue to develop those we have found, and are currently exploring several options to increase raw-material production in the U.S.

MADE IN CHINA

We make our products all over the world, including China, which has been rightly and roundly criticized for all sorts of shortcomings. China is not alone in this regard. Some of the other countries we work in also have poor to mixed records for protecting the environment and workers' rights. The record here in the U.S. is better, but not as good—in some cases not nearly as good—as either the E.U.' s or Japan's. We've made the choice not to disengage from countries on the basis of their policies. We believe in choosing factories wisely and in constructive engagement with others to lobby or work for change.

Of the 43 factories we currently contract with to make Patagonia products, 13 are in China and nine are in the U.S.[2] Far more of our products are made by those Chinese suppliers than they are by the U.S. factories because of their expertise and price, but we do work with factories in the United States when we can. In Los Angeles, we contract with a variety of suppliers, and we have long-term factory relationships in Texas and North Carolina. The factory we work with in Texas hires disabled workers, one of the reasons we work with them. Our new fishing crampons are made in Ventura, California, not far from Patagonia headquarters. As we become aware of new suppliers in the U.S., we investigate them.

---

[2] For the entire list, go to this link and scroll down the page: https://www.patagonia.com/reference -library.html.

TRANSPORTING GOODS & THE ENVIRONMENT

About half our sales today come from outside the United States, so manufacturing here, if we had the way to do so, would not necessarily result in environmental benefits from reduced transportation. We do think that strong long-term environmental arguments can be made on behalf of localism, of manufacturing closer to the point of purchase, which would include Japan, Europe, and a growing market for Patagonia products elsewhere in Asia. Two mitigating short-term factors: the enormity of change that would be required and the surprisingly low environmental cost of transportation, which accounts for less than 2% of the carbon footprint of our products.

Patagonia. (2013). Made in China. *The Footprint Chronicles*©. Retrieved May 18, 2019 from: https://www.patagonia.com/static/on/demandware.static/-/Library-Sites-PatagoniaShared/ default/dw29ab8345/PDF-US/Made_in_China_EN.pd.

PATAGONIA SUPPLIER WORKPLACE CODE OF CONDUCT

I. LAW AND CODE COMPLIANCE: Our suppliers are expected to comply with and will be monitored to: (1) all relevant and applicable laws and regulations of the country in which workers are employed including those at the federal, state/provincial and local community levels, (2) our Supplier Workplace Code of Conduct, (3) detailed Compliance Benchmark document, and (4) where applicable, Collective Bargaining Agreements. The Compliance Benchmarks identify specific requirements for meeting each Code standard. When differences or conflicts in standards arise, suppliers are expected to comply with the highest standard that is the most in favor of the employees.

II. CHILD LABOR: No person shall be employed under the age of 15 or under the age for completion of compulsory education, whichever is higher. Juvenile workers (ages 15–17) shall not perform work which, by its nature or the circumstances in which it is carried out, is likely to compromise their health, safety or morals. (ILO Convention 138 and 182)

III. FORCED LABOR: There shall be no use of forced labor, including prison, indentured, bonded, slave or other forms of forced labor. Acts of human trafficking are also prohibited. Suppliers are required to monitor any third-party entity which assists them in recruiting or hiring employees, to ensure that people seeking employment at their facility are not compelled to work through force, deception, intimidation, coercion or as a punishment for holding or expressing political views. (ILO Conventions 29, 105, 182)

IV. HARASSMENT, ABUSE AND DISCIPLINARY PRACTICES: Every employee shall be treated with respect and dignity. No employee shall be subject to any physical, sexual, psychological or verbal harassment or abuse or to monetary fines or embarrassing acts as a disciplinary measure.

V. DISCRIMINATION: No person shall be subject to any discrimination in any aspect of the employment, relationship including recruitment, hiring, compensation, benefits, work assignments, access to training, advancement, discipline, termination or retirement, on the basis of race, religious belief, color, gender, pregnancy, childbirth or related medical conditions, age, national origin, ancestry, sexual orientation, gender identification, physical or mental disability, medical condition, illness, genetic characteristics, family care, marital status, status as a veteran or qualified disabled veteran (in the USA only), caste, socio-economic situation, political opinion, union affiliation, ethnic group, illness or any other classification protected under applicable law. All employment decisions must be made based on the principle of equal employment opportunity, and shall include effective mechanisms to protect migrant, temporary or seasonal workers against any form of discrimination. (ILO Conventions 100 and 111)

VI. FREEDOM OF ASSOCIATION AND COLLECTIVE BARGAINING: Workers must be free to join organizations of their own choice. Suppliers shall recognize and respect the right of employees to freedom of association and collective bargaining. All suppliers must develop and fully implement effective grievance mechanisms which resolve internal industrial disputes, employee complaints, and ensure effective, respectful and transparent communication between employees, their representatives and management. (ILO Conventions 87, 98 and 135)

VII. EMPLOYMENT RELATIONSHIP: Employers shall adopt and adhere to rules and conditions of employment that respect workers and, at a minimum, safeguard their rights under national and international labor and social security laws and regulations.

VIII. WAGES AND BENEFITS: We seek and favor suppliers who progressively raise employee living standards through improved wage systems, benefits, welfare programs and other services, which exceed legal requirements and enhance quality of life. Every worker has a right to compensation for a regular work week that is sufficient to meet the worker's and their family's basic needs and provide some discretionary income. Employers shall pay wages which equal or exceed minimum wage or the appropriate prevailing wage, whichever is higher, comply with all legal requirements on wages, and provide any fringe benefits required by law and/or contract. Where compensation does not meet workers' basic needs and provide some discretionary income, each employer shall work with Patagonia and the Fair Labor Association (FLA) to take appropriate actions that seek to progressively realize a level of compensation that does. (ILO Conventions 26 and 131)

IX. OVERTIME WAGES: In addition to compensation for regular working hours, employees must be compensated for overtime hours at the rate legally required in the country of manufacture or, in those countries where such laws do not exist, at a rate exceeding the regular hourly compensation rate by at least 125%. (ILO Convention 1 and 30)

X. HOURS OF WORK: Suppliers shall not require workers to work more than the regular and overtime hours allowed by the law of the country where the workers are employed. The regular work week shall not exceed 48 hours or the maximum allowed by the law of the country of manufacture, whichever is less. Employers shall allow workers at least 24 consecutive hours of rest in every seven-day period. All overtime work shall be consensual. Employers shall not request overtime hours on a regular basis. The sum of regular and overtime hours in a week shall not exceed 60 hours or the maximum allowed by the law of the county of manufacture, whichever is less. (ILO Convention 1)

XI. HEALTH AND SAFETY: Suppliers shall provide a safe and healthy workplace to prevent accidents and injury to health arising out of, linked with, or occurring in the course of work or as a result of the operation of employers' facilities. The employer shall take a proactive approach to health and safety by implementing policies, systems and training designed to prevent accidents, injuries and protect worker health. (ILO Convention 155)

XII. ENVIRONMENT: Suppliers shall maintain written environmental policies and standards and must comply with all applicable environmental laws, our Code and Benchmarks, and agree to be monitored separately for environmental responsibility. Factories shall continuously monitor, and disclose to Patagonia, their energy and natural resource usage, emissions, discharges, carbon footprint and disposal of wastes and take a progressive approach to minimize negative impacts on the environment.

XIII. COMMUNITY: Patagonia encourages all suppliers and their employees to get involved in local social and environmental community charity efforts by volunteering time and/or providing other types of support. Patagonia has a solid history of supporting grass roots environmental non-profits and co-founded 1% for the Planet, an environmental advocacy organization in 2002. We seek long-term partnerships with suppliers that share these same philanthropic values.

XIV. SUBCONTRACTING: Patagonia does not permit subcontracting without our prior written approval. All salesman-sample and bulk production orders must be placed within facilities that have been pre-approved by Patagonia, without exception. Direct suppliers are required to continuously monitor approved subcontractors and sub-suppliers for social and environmental responsibility using standards that meet or exceed our Code and Benchmarks.

XV. ANIMAL WELFARE: Suppliers must respect animal welfare and work progressively towards adopting healthy and humane practices towards animals based on best available technology and standards.

XVI. TRACEABILITY: Patagonia and our suppliers are jointly responsible for ensuring social and environmental responsibility and the integrity of our product content claims from the farm through the finished goods factory level. The only way to work towards this goal is to have transparency and traceability into all levels of our supply chain. Patagonia requires suppliers to map and continuously track and monitor all locations in all levels of their supply chain and upon request provide transparency information into the owned and/or subcontracted farms, mills, plants, factories and other sites that are involved in the production of our products.

XVII. CODE COMMUNICATION: All suppliers are required to: (1) post the Patagonia Code standards and separate Patagonia grievance phone number document in a conspicuous place frequented by all employees in the local languages spoken by employees, supervisors and managers; (2) undertake annual, documented training efforts to educate current and new employees about the Patagonia Code standards and use of the Patagonia grievance phone number.

XVIII. QUALITY: Quality is the result of clarity, capable and well-integrated systems, and good communication. To achieve this, factories must have a clearly documented quality system and quality improvement plan. That system must include reliable "in process" and final finished goods audits and procedures that meet Patagonia's quality standards. These audits must be performed by a trained QA staff person provided by the factory. The QA staff person must be granted the autonomy and support he/she needs in order to provide an unbiased report on the quality of every shipment of finished goods. Compliance with our quality requirements is monitored by Patagonia's Quality Department.

CONTACT US: If suppliers are violating any of these Code elements, we would like to know about it. Please bring these issues to our attention by contacting us at the free phone number posted next to this Code or you can email us at social_responsibility@patagonia.com. Please feel free to write in your local language. All information we receive will be kept in strict confidence and your identity protected.

THIS CODE OF CONDUCT AND OUR SEPARATE GRIEVANCE PHONE NUMBER DOCUMENT MUST BE POSTED NEXT TO EACH OTHER WITHIN THE FACTORY IN A CONSPICUOUS, FREELY ACCESSIBLE AREA IN THE LOCAL LANGUAGE(S) OF THE EMPLOYEE

Patagonia. (n.d.). Supplier Workplace Code of Conduct. Retrieved May 18, 2019 from: https://www.patagonia.com/static/on/demandware.static/-/Library-Sites-PatagoniaShared/default/dw63489f7b/PDF-US/Patagonia_COC_English_02_13.pdf.

WALMART'S 15 QUESTIONS

Sustainability Supplier Assessment Questions

Energy and Climate *Reduce energy costs and greenhouse gas emissions*	1. Have you measured and taken steps to reduce your corporate greenhouse gas emissions? (Y/N) 2. Have you opted to report your greenhouse gas emissions and climate change strategy to the Carbon Disclosure Project (CDP)? (Y/N) 3. What are your total annual greenhouse gas emissions in the most recent year measured? (Enter total metric tons CO_2e, e.g., CDP 2009 Questionnaire, Questions 7–11, Scope 1 and 2 emissions) 4. Have you set publicly available greenhouse gas reduction targets? If yes, what are those targets? (Enter total metric tons and target date, e.g., CDP 2009 Questionnaire, Question 23)
Material Efficiency *Reduce waste and enhance quality*	Scores will be automatically calculated based on participation in the Packaging Scorecard in addition to the following: 5. If measured, please report total amount of solid waste generated from the facilities that produce your product(s) for Walmart for the most recent year measured. (Enter total lbs) 6. Have you set publicly available solid waste reduction targets? If yes, what are those targets? (Enter total lbs and target date) 7. If measured, please report total water use from the facilities that produce your product(s) for Walmart for the most recent year measured. (Enter total gallons) 8. Have you set publicly available water use reduction targets? If yes, what are those targets? (Enter total gallons and target date)

Continued

Nature and Resources *High quality, responsibly sourced raw materials*	9. Have you established publicly available sustainability purchasing guidelines for your direct suppliers that address issues such as environmental compliance, employment practices, and product/ingredient safety? (Y/N) 10. Have you obtained 3rd party certifications for any of the products that you sell to Walmart? If so, from the list of certifications below, please select those for which any of your products are, or utilize materials that are, currently certified.
People and Community *Vibrant, productive workplaces and communities*	11. Do you know the location of 100% of the facilities that produce your product(s)? (Y/N) 12. Before beginning a business relationship with a manufacturing facility, do you evaluate their quality of production and capacity for production? (Y/N) 13. Do you have a process for managing social compliance at the manufacturing level? (Y/N) 14. Do you work with your supply base to resolve issues found during social compliance evaluations and also document specific corrections and improvements? (Y/N) 15. Do you invest in community development activities in the markets you source from and/or operate within? (Y/N)

Walmart. (2009). Walmart Supplier Sustainability Assessment. Retrieved from: https://grist .files.wordpress.com/2011/11/4055.pdf.

CISCO ETHICS DECISION TREE

"Ask Yourself"—Ethics Decision Tree
Use the Ethics Decision Tree to assist you in determining the best course of action.

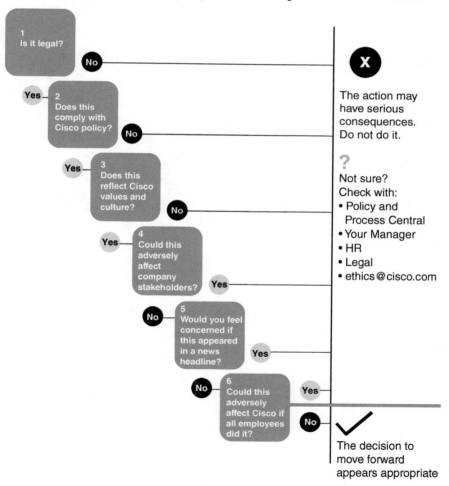

Cisco. (2018). Code of Business Conduct. Retrieved from: https://s2.q4cdn.com/ 951347115/files/doc_governance/code-of-business-conduct-fy18.pdf.

APPENDIX **4.2**

ETHISPHERE ETHICS QUOTIENT®
METHODOLOGY

Cisco Systems was listed in the Ethisphere World's Most Ethical Companies from 2008 to 2016. Beginning in 2015, Ethisphere made adjustments to its methodology. On its website, it states the following (Ethisphere, 2019a):

> *In 2015, the questionnaire was significantly revised across each assessment category, and in 2016 we made substantial additions in the areas of data privacy, cyber security and assessing an organization's ethical culture. 2017 saw an increased focus on diversity at the board and executive levels, compliance and ethics program structure (based on recent guidance from regulators), and how companies are evaluating their compliance and ethics programs. The updates for 2019 are extensive throughout all areas of the questionnaire.*

These are the five weighted categories of consideration in Ethisphere's Ethics Quotient® for 2019. Questions used in these areas change periodically based upon best practices, changes in regulations, and current expectations (Ethisphere, 2019b):

Ethisphere Methodology

- 15% Governance
- 10% Leadership and Reputation
- 35% Ethics and Compliance Program
- 20% Culture of Ethics
- 20% Corporate Citizenship and Responsibility

The list of categories and subcategories in 2019 were the following:

Governance (15%)

- Oversight
- Governance principles
- Risk management

Leadership and Reputation (10%)

- Legal compliance and ethical track record
- Ethical reputation in the marketplace
- Awards and accolades garnered
- Examples of leadership locally, nationally, and globally

Ethics and Compliance Program (35%)

- Program structure, responsibility, and resources
- Program oversight and tone at the top
- Written standards, training, and communication
- Due care, detection, monitoring, and auditing
- Enforcement and discipline

Culture of Ethics (20%)

- Efforts to establish ethical tone from top and middle
- Frequency with which culture is evaluated
- Methods and outcomes

Corporate Citizenship and Responsibility (20%)

- Sustainability, citizenship, and social responsibility
- Environmental stewardship
- Community involvement
- Corporate philanthropy
- Workplace impact and well-being
- Supply chain engagement and oversight

Ethisphere. (2019a). Frequently Asked Questions. Retrieved June 28, 2019 from: https://www.worldsmostethicalcompanies.com/faqs/.

Ethisphere. (2019b). Ethisphere Announces 128 World's Most Ethical Companies® for 2019. Retrieved June 28, 2019 from: https://www.worldsmostethicalcompanies.com/#methodology.

EXAMPLES OF APPROACHES TO STAKE-HOLDER ENGAGEMENT RELATIONSHIPS

Communication	Consultation	Dialogue	Partnerships
• Information sharing • Employee training • Project bulletins and letters to targeted audiences • Company brochures and reports • Internal and external newsletters • Websites • Technical briefings • Speeches, conference presentations, displays, handouts, and videos • Newsletters • Open houses and town hall meetings • Tours • Press releases, press conferences, media advertising	• Questionnaire surveys • Focus groups • Workplace assessments • Ad hoc stakeholder advisory meetings (e.g., community consultations) • Standing stakeholder advisory forums • Online feedback and discussion forums	• Multi-stakeholder forums • Advisory panels • Leadership summits • Virtual engagement on intranets and on the Internet	• Joint ventures • Local sustainable development projects • Multi-stakeholder initiatives • Alliances

Partridge, K., C. Jackson, D. Wheeler, and A. Zohar. (2005). Stakeholder Engagement Manual, Vol. 1: Guide to Practitioner's Perspectives. Cobourg, Canada: Stakeholder Research Associates Canada, Inc., UNEP and AccountAbility. Retrieved from: http://www.mas-business.com/docs/Vol%201%20Stakeholder%20Engagement%20Practitioners%20Perspectives.pdf.

CERES' 21ST CENTURY CORPORATION VISION: 20 KEY EXPECTATIONS

GOVERNANCE FOR SUSTAINABILITY

G1 Board Oversight

The Board of Directors will provide oversight and accountability for corporate sustainability strategy and performance. A committee of the board will assume specific responsibility for sustainability oversight within its charter.

G2 Management Accountability

The CEO and company management—from C-Suite executives to business unit and functional heads—will be responsible for achieving sustainability goals.

G3 Executive Compensation

Sustainability performance results are a core component of compensation packages and incentive plans for all executives.

G4 Corporate Policies and Management Systems

Companies will embed sustainability considerations into corporate policies and risk management systems to guide day-to-day decision making.

G5 Public Policy

Companies will clearly state their position on relevant sustainability public policy issues. Any lobbying will be done transparently and in a manner consistent with sustainability commitments and strategies.

STAKEHOLDER ENGAGEMENT

S1 Focus Engagement Activity

Companies will systematically identify a diverse group of stakeholders and regularly engage with them on sustainability risks and opportunities, including materiality analysis.

S2 Substantive Stakeholder Dialogue

Companies will engage stakeholders in a manner that is ongoing, in-depth, timely, and involves all appropriate parts of the business. Companies will disclose how they are incorporating stakeholder input into corporate strategy and business decision making.

S3 Investor Engagement

Companies will address specific sustainability risks and opportunities during annual meetings, analyst calls and other investor communications.

S4 C-Level Engagement

Senior executives will participate in stakeholder engagement processes to inform strategy, risk management and enterprise wide decision making.

DISCLOSURE

D1 Standards for Disclosure

Companies will disclose all relevant sustainability information using the Global Reporting Initiative (GRI) Guidelines as well as additional sector-relevant indicators.

D2 Disclosure In Financial Filings

Companies will disclose material sustainability issues in financial filings.

D3 Scope and Content

Companies will regularly disclose significant performance data and targets relating to their global direct operations, subsidiaries, joint ventures, products and supply chain. Disclosure will be balanced, covering challenges as well as positive impacts.

D4 Vehicles for Disclosure

Companies will release sustainability information through a range of disclosure vehicles, including stand-alone reports, annual reports, financial filings, websites and social media.

D5 Product Transparency

Companies will provide verified and standardized sustainability performance information about their products at point of sale and through other publicly available channels.

D6 Verification and Assurance

Companies will verify key sustainability performance data to ensure valid results and will have their disclosures reviewed by an independent, credible third party.

PERFORMANCE

P1 Operations

Companies will invest the necessary resources to achieve environmental neutrality and to demonstrate respect for human rights in their operations. Companies will measure and improve performance related to GHG emissions, energy efficiency, facilities and buildings, water, waste, and human rights.

1. Greenhouse Gas Emissions and Energy Efficiency: Companies will reduce greenhouse gas emissions by 25% from their 2005 baseline by 2020:

   - Improving energy efficiency of operations by at least 50%
   - Reducing electricity demand by at least 15%
   - Obtaining at least 30% of energy from renewable sources

2. Facilities and Buildings: Companies will ensure that at least 50% of their owned or leased facilities, and all new construction, will meet rigorous green buildings standards. When siting facilities, companies will follow best practices that incorporate sustainable land use and smart growth considerations.

3. Water Management: Companies will assess water-related impacts and risks and will set targets to improve water use and wastewater discharge, with priority given to operations in water stressed regions.

4. Eliminate Waste: Companies will design (or redesign, as appropriate) manufacturing and business processes as closed-loop systems, reducing toxic air emissions and hazardous and nonhazardous waste to zero.

5. Human Rights: Companies will regularly assess key risks related to human rights throughout their entire operations, and will employ management systems that are aligned with internal policies and support the implementation of universal standards.

P2 Supply Chain

Companies will require their suppliers to meet the same environmental and social standards as the company has established for itself. Companies will establish sustainable procurement criteria, catalyze improved supplier performance, and facilitate disclosure of suppliers' sustainability information.

1. Policies and Codes: Companies will set supply chain policies and codes aligned with overall social and environmental standards.

2. Align Procurement Practices: Companies will address sustainability performance in procurement criteria and contracting.

3. Engaging Suppliers: Companies will ensure that at least 75% of the company's Tier 1 and Tier 2 suppliers and 50% of Tier 3 suppliers meet the company's standards for sustainability performance.

4. Measurement and Disclosure: Companies will disclose a list of their Tier 1 and 2 suppliers and measure and disclose suppliers' sustainability performance.

P3 Transportation and Logistics

Companies will systematically minimize their sustainability impact by enhancing the resiliency of their logistics. Companies will prioritize low-impact transportation systems and modes, and address business travel and commuting.

1. Transportation Management: Companies will develop transportation criteria that incorporate distance requirements from site to market and establish decentralized and localized distribution networks.

2. Transportation Modes: Companies will review logistics to prioritize low-impact transportation modes.

3. Business Travel and Commuting: Companies will decrease greenhouse gas emissions from business travel and employee commuting by 50% from a baseline of 2005.

P4 Products and Services

Companies will design and deliver products and services that are aligned with sustainability goals by innovating business models, allocating R&D spend, designing for sustainability, communicating the impacts of products and services, reviewing marketing practices and advancing strategic collaborations.

1. Business Model Innovation: Companies will innovate business models to reduce material inputs and prioritize a transition to sustainable products and services.

2. R&D and Capital Investment: Companies will use sustainability as a primary filter through which all R&D and capital investments are made. 50% of the R&D investment will be focused on developing sustainability solutions.

3. Design for Sustainability: Companies will approach all product development and product management decisions with full consideration of the social and environmental impacts of the product throughout its life cycle.

4. Marketing Practices: Companies will align their marketing practices and product revenue targets with their sustainability goals and will market their designed-for-sustainability products and services with at least the same effort as their marketing of other products.

5. Strategic Collaborations: Companies will collaborate within and across sectors to innovate and scale sustainable products and services, and contribute to the development of open source solutions.

P5 Employees

Companies will make sustainability considerations a core part of recruitment, compensation and training, and will encourage sustainable lifestyle choices.

1. Recruitment and Retention: Companies will incorporate sustainability criteria into recruitment protocols, employee performance processes, compensation and incentives.

2. Training and Support: Companies will develop and implement formal training on key sustainability issues for all executives and employees, and facilitate coaching, mentoring and networks for sustainability knowledge sharing.

3. Promoting Sustainable Lifestyles: Companies will promote sustainable lifestyle choices across their community of employees through education and innovative employee benefit options.

Moffat, A., et al. (2010). The 21st Century Corporation: The Ceres Roadmap for Sustainability. Boston, MA: Ceres.

ALCOA MATERIAL TOPICS AND BOUNDARIES

Material Topic	Boundary
Economic Performance	Communities surrounding our operating locations, stockholders, lenders, financial analysts and investors globally
Greenhouse Gas Emissions	Communities surrounding our operating locations, government agencies and NGOs
Energy	Communities surrounding our operating locations, government agencies and NGOs
Water	Communities surrounding our operating locations (especially those in water-stressed regions of the world), government agencies and NGOs
Waste	Communities surrounding our operating locations, government agencies and NGOs
Biodiversity	Communities surrounding our operating locations, government agencies and NGOs
Health & Safety	Communities surrounding our operating locations and government agencies focused on health and safety in each country in which we operate
Local Communities	Communities surrounding our operating locations and NGOs

Alcoa. (2018). 2017 Alcoa Sustainability Report. Pittsburgh, PA: Alcoa Corporation.

UN GUIDING PRINCIPLES ON BUSINESS AND HUMAN RIGHTS

THE CORPORATE RESPONSIBILITY TO RESPECT HUMAN RIGHTS

A. FOUNDATIONAL PRINCIPLES.[1]

11. Business enterprises should respect human rights. This means that they should avoid infringing on the human rights of others and should address adverse human rights impacts with which they are involved.

12. The responsibility of business enterprises to respect human rights refers to internationally recognized human rights—understood, at a minimum, as those expressed in the International Bill of Human Rights and the principles concerning fundamental rights set out in the International Labour Organization's Declaration on Fundamental Principles and Rights at Work.

13. The responsibility to respect human rights requires that business enterprises:

(a) Avoid causing or contributing to adverse human rights impacts through their own activities, and address such impacts when they occur;

---

[1] The first 10 principles in this document are principles for governments, hence the list above starts with the number 11. Each of the principles listed here have commentary in the document referenced. I am listing the principles here to inspire you to go to the original document and read more.

(b) Seek to prevent or mitigate adverse human rights impacts that are directly linked to their operations, products or services by their business relationships, even if they have not contributed to those impacts.

14. The responsibility of business enterprises to respect human rights applies to all enterprises regardless of their size, sector, operational context, ownership and structure. Nevertheless, the scale and complexity of the means through which enterprises meet that responsibility may vary according to these factors and with the severity of the enterprise's adverse human rights impacts.

15. In order to meet their responsibility to respect human rights, business enterprises should have in place policies and processes appropriate to their size and circumstances, including:

    (a) A policy commitment to meet their responsibility to respect human rights;
    (b) A human rights due diligence process to identify, prevent, mitigate and account for how they address their impacts on human rights;
    (c) Processes to enable the remediation of any adverse human rights impacts they cause or to which they contribute.

B. OPERATIONAL PRINCIPLES

POLICY COMMITMENT

16. As the basis for embedding their responsibility to respect human rights, business enterprises should express their commitment to meet this responsibility through a statement of policy that:

    (a) Is approved at the most senior level of the business enterprise;
    (b) Is informed by relevant internal and/or external expertise;
    (c) Stipulates the enterprise's human rights expectations of personnel, business partners and other parties directly linked to its operations, products or services;
    (d) Is publicly available and communicated internally and externally to all personnel, business partners and other relevant parties;
    (e) Is reflected in operational policies and procedures necessary to embed it throughout the business enterprise.

HUMAN RIGHTS DUE DILIGENCE

17. In order to identify, prevent, mitigate and account for how they address their adverse human rights impacts, business enterprises should carry out human rights due diligence. The process should include assessing actual and potential human rights impacts, integrating and acting upon the findings, tracking responses, and communicating how impacts are addressed. Human rights due diligence:

    (a) Should cover adverse human rights impacts that the business enterprise may cause or contribute to through its own activities, or which may be directly linked to its operations, products or services by its business relationships;
    (b) Will vary in complexity with the size of the business enterprise, the risk of severe human rights impacts, and the nature and context of its operations;
    (c) Should be ongoing, recognizing that the human rights risks may change over time as the business enterprise's operations and operating context evolve.

18. In order to gauge human rights risks, business enterprises should identify and assess any actual or potential adverse human rights impacts with which they may be involved either through their own activities or as a result of their business relationships. This process should:

    (a) Draw on internal and/or independent external human rights expertise;
    (b) Involve meaningful consultation with potentially affected groups and other relevant stakeholders, as appropriate to the size of the business enterprise and the nature and context of the operation.

19. In order to prevent and mitigate adverse human rights impacts, business enterprises should integrate the findings from their impact assessments across relevant internal functions and processes, and take appropriate action.

    (a) Effective integration requires that:

        (i) Responsibility for addressing such impacts is assigned to the appropriate level and function within the business enterprise;

(ii) Internal decision making, budget allocations and oversight processes enable effective responses to such impacts.

(b) Appropriate action will vary according to:

(i) Whether the business enterprise causes or contributes to an adverse impact, or whether it is involved solely because the impact is directly linked to its operations, products or services by a business relationship;

(ii) The extent of its leverage in addressing the adverse impact.

20. In order to verify whether adverse human rights impacts are being addressed, business enterprises should track the effectiveness of their response. Tracking should:

(a) Be based on appropriate qualitative and quantitative indicators;

(b) Draw on feedback from both internal and external sources, including affected stakeholders.

21. In order to account for how they address their human rights impacts, business enterprises should be prepared to communicate this externally, particularly when concerns are raised by or on behalf of affected stakeholders. Business enterprises whose operations or operating contexts pose risks of severe human rights impacts should report formally on how they address them. In all instances, communications should:

(a) Be of a form and frequency that reflect an enterprise's human rights impacts and that are accessible to its intended audiences;

(b) Provide information that is sufficient to evaluate the adequacy of an enterprise's response to the particular human rights impact involved;

(c) In turn not pose risks to affected stakeholders, personnel or to legitimate requirements of commercial confidentiality.

REMEDIATION

22. Where business enterprises identify that they have caused or contributed to adverse impacts, they should provide for or cooperate in their remediation through legitimate processes.

ISSUES OF CONTEXT

23. In all contexts, business enterprises should:

(a) Comply with all applicable laws and respect internationally recognized human rights, wherever they operate;

(b) Seek ways to honour the principles of internationally recognized human rights when faced with conflicting requirements;

(c) Treat the risk of causing or contributing to gross human rights abuses as a legal compliance issue wherever they operate.

24. Where it is necessary to prioritize actions to address actual and potential adverse human rights impacts, business enterprises should first seek to prevent and mitigate those that are most severe or where delayed response would make them irremediable.

United Nations. (2011). *Guiding Principles on Business and Human Rights: Implementing the United Nations "Protect, Respect and Remedy" Framework.* New York, NY and Geneva, Switzerland: United Nations. Retrieved from: https://www.ohchr.org/Documents/Publications/GuidingPrinciplesBusinessHR_EN.pdf.

S&P 500® CORPORATE SUSTAINABILITY REPORTING, 2011–2015

The following chart shows the increase in sustainability reporting by S&P 500® companies, indicating that such reporting has now gone mainstream.

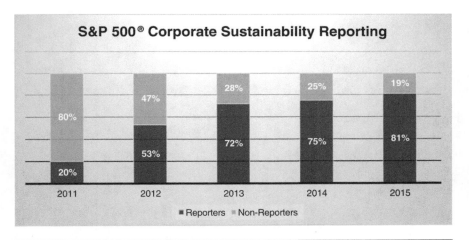

S&P 500® Corporate Sustainability Reporting

Governance & Accountability Institute, Inc. (2016). "Flash Report: 81% of S&P 500 Companies Published Sustainability Reports in 2015." Retrieved from: https://www.ga -institute.com/press-releases/article/flash-report-eighty-one-percent-81-of-the-sp-500 -index-companies-published-corporate-sustainabi.html.

APPENDIX **8.2**

ING BUILDING BLOCKS TO A LOW CARBON SOCIETY

Contribute to a Low-Carbon and Self-Reliant Society

Climate Business	Climate Resilience	Social Business	Inclusion and Empowerment
Future-proofing Wholesale Banking clients by growing Climate Finance and Industry ESG leaders	Steer portfolio to align with the well-below two-degree scenario	Future-proofing Wholesale Banking clients by growing Social Impact Finance and Industry ESG leaders	Using our data analytics to improve the financial health of our customers (Financial Empowerment)
Future-proofing SME/Mid-Corp clients	Future-proof homeowners by making their houses more sustainable	Growing Sustainable Assets under Management	Partnering to help consumers in smarter decision making (Think Forward Initiative)
Growing Sustainable Assets under Management	Introducing policies, such as our sharpened coal policy	Partnering to protect human rights (DBSA agreement)	Empowering adolescents through Power for Youth programme
Developing and collaborating on innovative banking solutions	Decreasing our operational footprint to well below 2 degrees		Empowering female colleagues through diversity programme
Partnering to accelerate circular economy (Ellen MacArthur Foundation/WEF)	Recognise, understand and find solutions to address water stress		

ING. (n.d.). "Our direction." Retrieved May 21, 2019 from: https://www.ing.com/Sustainability/Our-direction.htm.

NESTLÉ FRAMING OF CREATING SHARED VALUE (CSV)

Framing our CSV approach

Our purpose: enhancing quality of life and contributing to a healthier future

For individuals and families	For our communities	For the planet
Enabling healthier and happier lives	Helping develop thriving, resilient communities	Stewarding resources for future generations
Our 2030 ambition is to help 50 million children lead healthier lives	**Our 2030 ambition is to improve 30 million livelihoods in communities directly connected to our business activities**	**Our 2030 ambition is to strive for zero environmental impact in our operations**
Offering tastier and healthier choices	Rural development and enhancing rural livelihoods	Caring for water
Inspiring people to lead healthier lives	Respecting and promoting human rights	Acting on climate change
Building, sharing and applying nutrition knowledge	Promoting decent employment and diversity	Safeguarding our environment
Related CSV impact area	**Related CSV impact areas**	**Related CSV impact areas**
Nutrition	Rural development Human rights Our people	Water Environmental sustainability

Our commitments	We have 41 commitments to hold ourselves publicly accountable for our performance, and we report our progress against them every year. All our public commitments are directly aligned with our corporate purpose and the majority are supported by specific objectives towards 2020.
Our values	Underpinning all our efforts are our company values, rooted in respect, respect for ourselves, respect for others, respect for diversity and respect for the future.

Nestlé. (2018). *Nestlé in Society: Creating Shared Value and meeting our commitments 2017.* Vevey, Switzerland: Nestlé Group. Retrieved from: https://www.nestle.com/asset-library/documents/library/documents/corporate_social_responsibility/nestle-csv-full-report-2017-en.pdf.

ANDREW WINSTON BIG PIVOT STRATEGIES

THE BIG PIVOT STRATEGIES

To be resilient, companies must transform their strategies in three ways: They must rethink their vision, embracing radical innovation and a long-term mindset; redefine their valuation methods to account for unpriced costs and benefits; and pursue new kinds of partnerships to achieve goals beyond the reach of individual firms.

VISION
FIGHT SHORT-TERMISM
SET SCIENCE-BASED GOALS
PURSUE HERTICAL INNOVATION

INSPIRE CUSTOMERS TO USE LESS
COLLABORATE RADICALLLY
BECOME A LOBBYIST

BUILD A RESILIENT COMPANY

CHANGE INCENTIVES
REDEFINE ROI
VALUE NATURAL CAPITAL

PARTNERS

VALUATION

Winston, A. (April, 2014). Resilience in a Hotter World: Extreme weather and rising demand for resources call for a fundamentally new strategy. *Harvard Business Review*. Retrieved from: https://hbr.org/2014/04/resilience-in-a-hotter-world. **175**

KAPLAN AND NORTON: RESOURCES FOR STRATEGY AND PLANNING

This list of resources was contained in the article referenced at the end of Chapter 10: Kaplan and Norton. (2007). "Mastering the Management System." *Harvard Business Review*. https://hbr.org/2008/01/mastering-the-management-system.

A MANAGEMENT SYSTEM TOOL KIT

Where to learn more about the concepts and frameworks described in this article.

DEVELOP THE STRATEGY

Competitive Strategy

- Michael E. Porter, *Competitive Advantage: Creating and Sustaining Superior Performance*, Free Press, 1985 (republished with a new introduction, 1998).
- Michael E. Porter, *Competitive Strategy: Techniques for Analyzing Industries and Competitors*, Free Press, 1980 (republished with a new introduction, 1998).
- Michael E. Porter, "What Is Strategy?", *Harvard Business Review* November–December 1996.
- Chris Zook and James Allen, *Profit from the Core: Growth Strategy in an Era of Turbulence*, Harvard Business School Press, 2001.

Resource-Based Strategy

- Jay B. Barney, *Gaining and Sustaining Competitive Advantage—3rd edition*, Prentice-Hall, 2006.

- Jay B. Barney and Delwyn N. Clark, *Resource-Based Theory: Creating and Sustaining Competitive Advantage*, Oxford University Press, 2007.
- David J. Collis and Cynthia A. Montgomery, "Competing on Resources: Strategy in the 1990s", *Harvard Business Review* July–August 1995.
- Gary Hamel and C.K. Prahalad, *Competing for the Future*, Harvard Business School Press, 1994.

Blue Ocean Strategy

- W. Chan Kim and Renée Mauborgne, *Blue Ocean Strategy: How to Create Uncontested Market Space and Make the Competition Irrelevant*, Harvard Business School Press, 2005.

Disruptive Strategy

- Clayton M. Christensen and Michael E. Raynor, *The Innovator's Solution: Creating and Sustaining Successful Growth*, Harvard Business School Press, 2003.

Emergent Strategy

- Gary Hamel, "Strategy Innovation and the Quest for Value", *MIT Sloan Management Review* Winter, 1998.
- Henry Mintzberg, "Crafting Strategy", *Harvard Business Review* July–August 1987.

Translate the Strategy

- Robert S. Kaplan and David P. Norton, *The Strategy-Focused Organization: How Balanced Scorecard Companies Thrive in the New Business Environment*, Harvard Business School Press, 2000.
- Robert S. Kaplan and David P. Norton, *Strategy Maps: Converting Intangible Assets into Tangible Outcomes*, Harvard Business School Press, 2004.
- Robert S. Kaplan and David P. Norton, *The Execution Premium: Linking Strategy to Operations for Competitive Advantage*, Harvard Business School Press, 2008.

PLAN OPERATIONS

Process Improvement

- Wayne W. Eckerson, *Performance Dashboards: Measuring, Monitoring, and Managing Your Business*, John Wiley & Sons, 2006.
- Michael Hammer, *Beyond Reengineering: How the Process-Centered Organization Is Changing Our Work and Our Lives*, HarperBusiness, 1996.
- Peter S. Pande, Robert P. Neuman, and Roland R. Cavanagh, *The Six Sigma Way: How GE, Motorola, and Other Top Companies Are Honing Their Performance*, McGraw-Hill, 2000.
- James P. Womack, Daniel T. Jones, and Daniel Roos, *The Machine That Changed the World: The Story of Lean Production*, Macmillan, 1990.

Budgeting and Planning Resource Capacity

- Jeremy Hope and Robin Fraser, *Beyond Budgeting: How Managers Can Break Free from the Annual Performance Trap*, Harvard Business School Press, 2003.
- Robert S. Kaplan and Steven R. Anderson, *Time-Driven Activity-Based Costing: A Simpler and More Powerful Path to Higher Profits*, Harvard Business School Press, 2007.

Test and Adapt Strategy

- Dennis Campbell, Srikant Datar, Susan L. Kulp, and V.G. Narayanan, "Testing Strategy Formulation and Implementation Using Strategically Linked Performance Measures", HBS Working Paper, 2006.
- Thomas H. Davenport and Jeanne G. Harris, *Competing on Analytics: The New Science of Winning*, Harvard Business School Press, 2007.
- Anthony J. Rucci, Steven P. Kirn, and Richard T. Quinn, "The Employee-Customer-Profit Chain at Sears", *Harvard Business Review* January–February 1998.

Kaplan, M. and M. Norton. (2007). "Mastering the Management System." Harvard Business Review. https://hbr.org/2008/01/mastering-the-management-system.

BSR AND UNGC: BUILDING THE BUSINESS CASE FOR SUPPLY CHAIN SUSTAINABILITY

BUSINESS DRIVERS
FOR SUPPLY CHAIN SUSTAINABILITY

Managing business risks	Realizing efficiencies	Creating sustainable products
▶ Minimize business disruption from environmental, social, and economic impacts ▶ Protect company's reputation and brand value	▶ Reduce cost of material inputs, energy, and transportation ▶ Increase labor productivity ▶ Create efficiency across supply chains	▶ Meet evolving customer and business partner requirements ▶ Innovate for changing market

GOVERNANCE, MANAGEMENT, TRANSPARENCY

UNGC and BSR. (2010). "Supply Chain Sustainability: A Practical Guide for Continuous Improvement." Available at: https://www.bsr.org/reports/BSR_UNGC_SupplyChainReport.pdf.

UNGC AND BSR: TOOLS FOR ENGAGING WITH SUPPLIERS ON SUSTAINABILITY

Deep
Engagement

PARTNERSHIP
Support supplier
ownership to address
the root causes of poor
sustainability performance

**REMEDIATION &
CAPABILITY BUILDING**
Ask suppliers to address issues of poor
performance. Provide training, resources,
and support to improve sustainability
management and performance.

Broad
Engagement

MONITORING & EVALUATION
Ask suppliers to self-assess their sustainability performance.
Conduct on-site evaluations of performance.

SETTING EXPECTATIONS
Communicate about your sustainability expectations to suppliers.
Incorporate expectations, including the code of conduct, into contracts.

UNGC and BSR. (2010). "Supply Chain Sustainability: A Practical Guide for Continuous Improvement." Available at: https://www.bsr.org/reports/BSR_UNGC_SupplyChainReport.

SHAREHOLDER PROPOSALS IN 2019

The following chart shows the percentage of various types of shareholder proposals filed in 2019. This can help you understand what is currently material to public company shareholders at this time.

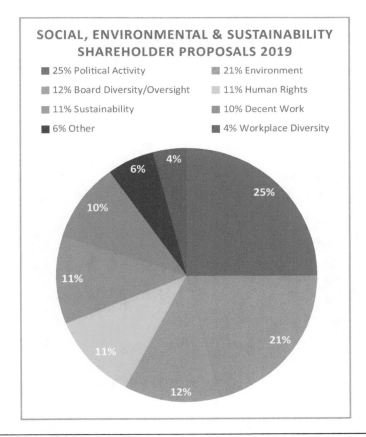

SOCIAL, ENVIRONMENTAL & SUSTAINABILITY SHAREHOLDER PROPOSALS 2019

- 25% Political Activity
- 21% Environment
- 12% Board Diversity/Oversight
- 11% Human Rights
- 11% Sustainability
- 10% Decent Work
- 6% Other
- 4% Workplace Diversity

Welsh, H. and M. Passoff. (2019). Proxy Preview: Helping Shareholders Vote Their Values. Proxy Preview. Retrieved from: https://www.proxypreview.org/2019/report-cover.

KPMG SURVEY OF CORPORATE RESPONSIBILITY REPORTING

QUANTITATIVE TRENDS IN CORPORATE RESPONSIBILITY REPORTING

- **CR reporting is standard practice for large and mid-cap companies around the world**
  - ▫ Around three-quarters of the companies studied in this survey (4,900) issue CR reports.

- **All industry sectors show a healthy rate of CR reporting**
  - ▫ For the first time in the history of this survey, every sector has a reporting rate of 60% or more.

- **Latin America has seen a surge in CR reporting in the last two years**
  - ▫ Driven by regulation, foreign investor demand and the need to build and protect public trust.

- **Most of the world's biggest companies now integrate financial and non-financial data in their annual financial reports (78 percent)**
  - ▫ Suggesting they believe CR information is relevant for investors.

- **Assurance of CR data has more than doubled among the G250 in the last 12 years (now 67 percent of reports)**
  - ▫ Indicating that the largest companies see value in promoting the reliability of this information. Assurance is also increasing at a steady rate among N100 companies.

- **"Integrated Reporting" has taken off in Japan, Brazil, Mexico, and Spain.**

- **GRI remains the most popular framework for CR reporting.**
  - Around two thirds of reports analyzed in this survey apply the GRI G4 Guidelines or Standards.

KMPG. (2017). The Road Ahead: KMPG Survey of Corporate Responsibility Reporting 2017. Geneva, Switzerland: KMPG International Cooperative.

TUNNELING THROUGH
THE COST BARRIER

In chapter 6 of *Natural Capitalism*, the authors discuss the concept of "tunneling through the cost barrier." This is done by thinking beyond normal solutions to combine resources in a way that reduces costs overall. For example, investing in the best available insulation and insulated windows, and designing a building to take the best advantage of sun for heating and cooling, can mean the building may need a smaller furnace or air cooling system—or maybe none at all. This additional investment beyond what is normally considered reasonable results in less expense for efficiencies and greater energy savings.

At the Rocky Mountain Institute, this whole systems approach to design and engineering is key to their success in resource management and energy efficiency. In their work to remodel the Empire State Building, investments in super insulated windows, increased building insulation, and smart thermostats made the building so efficient that heating and cooling demands were greatly reduced. The result avoided the cost of digging up Fifth Avenue to replace the old boilers and reduced the cost of operating the building.

The figures below depict how this idea is expressed. Figure 14.1A shows the point where most projects meet a barrier of efficiency investments due to diminishing returns on investment.

Figure 14.1B shows how continued investment beyond the considered limit can trigger savings in other areas, ultimately reducing the costs overall—sometimes to a net savings.

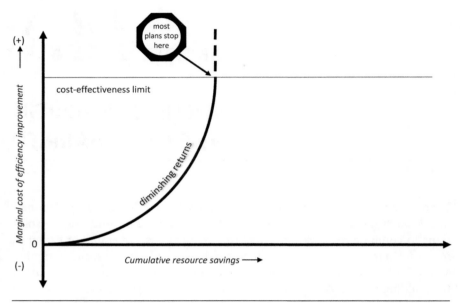

Figure 14.1A   Business as Usual